DREAM BIG

DREAM BIG

Know What You Want, Why You Want It,

and What You're Going to Do About It

BOB GOFF

NELSON
BOOKS

An Imprint of Thomas Nelson

Published in Nashville, Tennessee, by Nelson Books, an imprint of Thomas Nelson. Nelson Books and Thomas Nelson are registered trademarks of HarperCollins Christian Publishing, Inc.

Represented by Alive Literary Agency, www.aliveliterary.com.

Thomas Nelson titles may be purchased in bulk for educational, business, fundraising, or sales promotional use. For information, please e-mail SpecialMarkets@ThomasNelson.com.

Scripture quotations are taken from the Holy Bible, New International Version®, NIV®. Copyright © 1973, 1978, 1984, 2011 by Biblica, Inc.® Used by permission of Zondervan. All rights reserved worldwide. www.Zondervan.com. The "NIV" and "New International Version" are trademarks registered in the United States Patent and Trademark Office by Biblica, Inc.®

Any Internet addresses, phone numbers, or company or product information printed in this book are offered as a resource and are not intended in any way to be or to imply an endorsement by Thomas Nelson, nor does Thomas Nelson vouch for the existence, content, or services of these sites, phone numbers, companies, or products beyond the life of this book.

Some names and identifying details have been altered to protect people's identities.

ISBN 978-1-4002-1950-6 (eBook)
ISBN 978-1-4002-1949-0 (HC)
ISBN 978-1-4002-2097-7 (IE)

Library of Congress Control Number: 2020935464

Printed in the United States of America
20 21 22 23 24 LSC 10 9 8 7 6 5 4 3 2 1

This book is dedicated to all the people who stand in the middle of my life. Sweet Maria, Lindsey, Jon, Richard, Ashley, Adam, and all the people they love the most. Thank you for living lives that inspire me to pursue my dreams and point me toward more lasting ambitions than the ones I would have come up with by myself.

To you, the reader, I hope you will dedicate yourself to constantly changing into a more authentic version of yourself. Charles Dickens once famously said, "There are books of which the backs and covers are by far the best parts." I've read a couple of those. Perhaps you have too. I hope you'll decide this book has a middle worth reading. Don't settle for the cover story. It's in the middle of our lives where all the good stuff happens. As you read these pages, dig deep and find what's in here for you. All of heaven is counting on you to show up and fully engage your beautiful life.

CONTENTS

Introduction ix

Part 1: Getting Ready to Dream Big

1. Don't Go Alone 3
2. Thermometer 7
3. Get Under the Ice Cap 13
4. Who Are You? 21
5. Where Are You? 27
6. What Do You Want? 31
7. Chase the Jeep 37
8. Getting to the "New" Part 45
9. Sleepwalking 51
10. One Hundred Calls a Day 59
11. Sea Otters 65
12. Finale 73
13. Comparison Is a Punk 83

Part 2: Set Absurd Expectations

14. Gather Your Leaves 91
15. Sizing Up 99
16. Get the Sticks Before the Drums 109

Part 3: Explore Opportunities

17. Keep the Moon in the Window 117
18. The Number for the White House Is (202) 456-1414 . . 123

Part 4: Clear the Path

19. Hostage Negotiation 131
20. Give It a Quarter Twist 137
21. Be a Quitter 143

Part 5: Take Action

22. Living on the Edge of Yikes 153
23. 10:34–10:35 159
24. One Thousand Words a Day 167

Part 6: Expect Setbacks

25. Pick the Vespa 175
26. Three Epic Fails 183

Part 7: Sustain Belief and Land the Plane

27. Check Your Ropes 191
28. Ground Effect 197
29. Matters of the Heart 205

Epilogue 213

The Dream Big Framework: Reflection Questions
    and Action Ideas 215

Acknowledgments 233

About the Author 235

Connect with Bob 237

INTRODUCTION

What will you do with your
one extraordinary life?

I have been teaching as an adjunct professor at Pepperdine Law School for more than a decade. It's a place filled with bright, ambitious law students, many of whom have had a lot of life break in their direction. I also teach a class at San Quentin State Prison. My class there is filled with men who are felons, and their misdeeds have exacted a high price from them—namely, their freedom. I learn quite a bit from both sets of students, but the contrast between them cannot be overlooked. There is an authenticity that brokenness can refine in our lives if we'll let it. Ironically, the guys with the life sentences often seem to be living freer lives than the law students with all the opportunities. Their brokenness ultimately led them to a personal freedom, even behind bars.

Have you ever wondered why some people achieve so much with their lives and others don't? One person starts with no money, some terrible circumstances, and seems to be the happiest, most fulfilled and self-aware person you've ever met. Another person is born with a trust fund, good looks, and endless apparent opportunities, and yet they lead a sad, self-absorbed, meaningless life. What happened to allow some people to make the shift and others to miss the ramp? Some people seem to move from success to success, while others seem to be stuck in a loop of pain and sadness and distress. Some people also have a rich and vibrant faith that is taking them places, while others believe the same things just as much but seem stuck struggling with their beliefs and how to reconcile them with their lives.

In short, why is it some people live inspired lives and others can't? How come some people glide through life and others grind it out? Why is it that some people seem to be living three times more than a normal life, and others feel like they are only living half of one? These are all questions most of us ask ourselves at some point. Where do you think you fit on the spectrum? Don't shade it, fake it, or sweat the answer. Just get real about it. Here's why: we need to figure out where we are before we can plot a course forward.

The fact is no map will take us where God wants to lead us. We are all off-roading most of the time. Yet there are plenty of clues out there for living the big and meaningful life that Jesus talked to His friends about. Instead of telling them to look for a plan, He pointed them toward their much bigger purposes. In the pages that follow, let's figure out where your purposes are and then hatch a plan to get there.

I've written a few books, and some of the stories probably made you laugh, while others made you cry. I want this book to make you think. In the pages that follow, I hope you'll figure out where your purposes lie and then chart a course to get there.

When I was out of college and living alone, I had a closet in my house where I would throw the things that didn't have a specific place to go. Naturally, this closet quickly became a huge, disorganized, impenetrable pile of debris. Everything in there was evidently important enough to acquire at some point and even valuable enough to keep, yet none of these things remained accessible to me anymore because there was no order to them. As a result, a whole lot of items, with individual value, were collectively worthless because I couldn't get at them.

Our lives are not much different. We gather experiences, emotions, knowledge, and self-awareness. We amass pains, triumphs, disappointments, and wisdom. Without some shelves to put them on, though, we can't access these things or what they've taught us to help us move forward. These experiences and "aha!" moments are the stuff you'll need to access as you figure out what your next moves are going to be in the direction of your ambitions. Put aside the self-help talk. What you need is a good set of shelving to access what you've already experienced and a willingness to reflect on what you find there.

It took 220 years after the pencil was invented for someone to invent the eraser. I'm glad they did because I've erased in my life much more than I've kept. We all get to do this. We take what we've written about ourselves, what we truly believe God thinks of us, and decide what to keep and what to erase. We're not the only author of our lives either. Like the ones who have signed the pages of a high school yearbook, other people who have intersected our journey have written over us too. Some of what they said is true and beautiful and lasting. Other things not so much. "Never change" was written in my yearbook by at least a dozen people. It's the worst advice I've ever received. We're supposed to change constantly—into kinder, humbler, more faithful versions of our old selves. This change and growth happens when we sort out the truth from the lies in our lives. Here's some great news. The next version of you is the one who will pursue the ambitions all the previous versions were unable to accomplish.

Our understanding of who we are and how God sees us is worth all the time and energy we'll put into the task. The trick is figuring out what is true after all the distractions, misstatements, and misunderstandings have been eliminated from our lives. Here's what makes it worth it: when we sort through all the words written by ourselves and others, and when we discard what isn't true or doesn't matter anymore, we'll find the clarity we need to choose the desires worth pursuing. What's left over will be your truest, most beautiful, and lasting ambitions. That's what this book is all about.

My faith has shaped my worldview and plays a big part in my ambitions. I decided to make my first and last ambition to love God and the people I come across without an agenda. I certainly haven't arrived, but I'm somewhere along the way of getting there. You are too.

My relationships play a big role too. Some people are easy to connect with. If you want to achieve great things, find a couple of these people to do life with. Also find a couple of difficult people to engage with love. Don't make them projects; make them friends. This is where you'll grow. If you do these things, I promise you will lead a purposeful and meaningful life. Sure, it will be complicated at times, and you'll mess it up more than once, but your purpose will never become clearer. I know this because if you go deep with a few people and stay close to those who rub you the wrong way, you will have accomplished the ambitions Jesus said were always worth the effort.

While no efforts of yours or mine will be more important than loving God and the people around us, our ambitions can be much broader, more expansive, and more varied than this. I want to talk about those things too.

Achieving your ambitions isn't going to come easy, and it won't be cheap. Don't bail out. Will you have setbacks along the way? Of course you will. The reason is simple: you are you and life is life. Stay the course. We've brought leaders together in countries riddled with conflict only to have our meetings raided. I've been detained, held in jail, and even kicked out of a country for freeing children held in brothels. We've started schools in war zones that failed completely and other schools that shouldn't have worked but did. Don't be put off by the difficulties you'll face; remember the reason why you started. Keep your ambitions and your life's purpose in mind. Why? Because our lives are on-the-job training for eternity.

If ambitions had two handles, they would be love and hope. There have never been two forces in the world more powerful than these. Much of life involves simply grabbing ahold of love and hope and never letting go.

One of the writers in the Bible named Paul nailed it when he said, "The only thing that counts is faith expressing itself through love." I agree. It's easy to mistake faith with all the doctrine you believe to be true. Faith, however, is what you do about what you believe. It's easy for most of us to hope big things for other people. It's beautiful and right, and we should keep doing lots of that. This book is about hoping a couple of things for ourselves as well, then engaging our most important ambitions with confidence and a strategy so we can release those ambitions into the world.

Setting aside a time for personal reflection about who you are, why you think what you think, and why you do what you do is the heavy lifting you'll need to do if you want to accomplish things in your life you haven't been able to yet. I'm not advocating you go on a hedonistic bender and make everything about yourself. You will find nothing less fulfilling than making everything about you. This book is about self-discovery, not self-help. It's not about simply having dreams. Dreams are too easy. Even my dog wags its tail when it's asleep. I want you to become fully awake to your biggest and most worthwhile ambitions by becoming fully awake to yourself and your God-given purposes.

All this requires developing a new way of thinking. To do this you're going to need to carve a new groove in your brain so you can get after your ambitions rather than just push them around on the plate like a bunch of peas. Carving a new groove in your brain is like blowing up a balloon. A big balloon. Sometimes your head starts spinning after a while when you think about your ambitions. Take some breaks. Rest is holy. Get as much as you need, but know when it's time to be fully awake and get back to work. If we're going to get after some of your unexecuted ambitions, we need to take that new groove you're carving and go Grand Canyon on it. Doing this is going to take some effort, but hey, do it anyway.

Let me get this out there. God is over the moon about you. Honest. I've asked Him. He's not grimacing at your past failures; He's smiling at the bright future you have with Him. As you pursue your ambitions, rest in knowing that heaven is simply nuts about you and can't wait for you to get there. That said, you've got some time right here, so make good use of it. Making eternity one of your biggest ambitions is terrific, but what if we use this desire to better understand your short time here on earth and what you'll do next with your life.

I'm really excited you chose to pick up this book. It's a reflection of the life I've tried to live for decades. I've had a couple of successes and plenty of failures. I'll let you know about both. I have tried to tease together my best explanation for why these things happened and what I learned when they did. While I hope you have a blast reading this book, know that there is a process and a journey baked into its pages. If all we had in the end was a bunch of words, what good would that do us? We need a path, and I hope this book provides one that moves you toward your ambitions. I also hope you'll find your deeper purposes in these pages. Let's have some fun together, sure. But don't get distracted and think that a good time is all we're about. We want to be the kind of people who release amazing things into the world and are willing to do whatever it takes to make it happen.

To this end, there is a section in the back of the book with some questions for you to think about and some actions you can take to move toward your dream. I hope you'll have a pen in your hand while you read. Maybe get a journal, too, dedicated to the process in this book. I've based the questions and the words you'll read in these pages on a live workshop I've been doing called Dream Big. We've had leaders from our country and Middle Eastern countries, Grammy-winning musicians, megachurch pastors, stay-at-home moms, billionaires, and broke college students attend. I've watched these and thousands of others follow the ideas and principles we'll discuss as they move forward with their ambitions. This book is my attempt to show you what those thousands of others have learned for themselves—that there is a path to discover and release your most beautiful and lasting ambitions into the world. Don't settle for anything less, because God says you're worth it.

Part 1

GETTING READY TO DREAM BIG

Chapter 1

DON'T GO ALONE

If you are serious about your dream, surround yourself with people who love you well.

There she was. Maria. She wasn't "Sweet Maria" yet because we didn't know each other. She was definitely still sweet, but I hadn't gotten the chance to call her that. When I first saw her across the room thirty-five years ago, I was immediately smitten. I would have jumped out of a moving car to meet her. It took a while, but she figured out I liked her. Perhaps it was the list of names I created for our children and gave her a short time later. Eventually, she reluctantly learned my name. She even said it once or twice, or at least I thought she did, because she was usually walking away. I remember her saying things like, "Thanks for the invitation, Bob, but no," and "I'm sorry, Bob, but I'm busy that year," and "Bob, are the pair of panda bears in my yard from you?" I think I'm an acquired taste.

After way too long, Maria started liking me back. When this happened, it was like the part in *The Wizard of Oz* when everything goes from black and white to color for the first time. It was in my pursuit of Maria that I learned the importance of having an ambition and staying after it, no matter how big or impossible it seemed. I knew what I wanted, why I wanted it, and I decided what I was going to do about it. There is a silent flip of a switch that happens when we make this determination about something we want. It's the point where we move from just thinking about an ambition to actually doing something about it.

I clinched the deal when I invited her rock climbing with me. I had her tied to the end of the rope, and before she started climbing, she looked up at me and saw me confidently holding the rope. She told me later she realized in that moment she could trust me with her life. Pursuing your ambitions will take an equally big dollop of trust. God's got you. Take the risk. It's worth it.

Eventually Sweet Maria said yes, and we made a few kids to go with my list of names. It's thirty-five years later, and whatever I'm good at these days, it's because Sweet Maria Goff is better at it. One of the many things she's good at is knowing herself and finding joy in her unique set of gifts, abilities, and desires. She doesn't compare her abilities and ambitions to anyone else's. She knows that God doesn't compare what He creates. She also knows what she wants, why she wants it, and what she's going to do about it. Having this kind of clarity is rare and beautiful and unstoppable. Aim for this in your life and you will find great joy.

Sweet Maria and I could not be more different. I love meeting new people, and the more of them in a room the better. Maria, on the other hand, thinks having me in the room is a lot of people and finds her purpose in being fully present with our family. Not many people get to see her. It's like seeing a unicorn. She simply doesn't need or want the attention.

She wrote a bestselling book once. Instead of going on a book tour or having a release party and inviting thousands of our friends, she ordered a medium pizza for the family and we made root beer floats at home. The way she lives her life is a daily reminder to me that our purpose is not found in another person's validation. It's not found in familiarity or approval or popularity either. It is discovered somewhere far deeper within us. Maria lives her life solely and sacrificially for our family and a handful of friends. She not only helps us better understand the complex world we live in, but she also helps me get ready each day so I don't leave the house with one pant leg tucked into my sock.

I'll admit, it's a lot of work to live with a guy who acts like he's sponsored by Red Bull. They call my drink of choice at the local coffee stand "Goffee." It's two shots of energy drink and three shots of espresso. I may die young, but I'll be wide awake when I do. Sweet Maria likes to say I'm the balloon and she's the string. This beautifully describes the right kind of codependence. If you want to achieve your ambitions, don't be all balloon and no string in your life. We need to be anchored in God and tied to one another.

Being different isn't always easy. Perhaps you've felt like you were different than your friends or family. That's a good thing, and we're going to need to settle into who God created us to be if we're going to move ahead. To be purposeful and at ease with who we are, we're going to need to be incredibly truthful with ourselves and the people around us, which is something Sweet Maria lives out every day. If she told me ghosts pooped Tic Tacs, I'm certain I'd believe her. In these pages it will seem like you're reading my thoughts, but you're actually reading what I've learned from her.

I'm always the optimist, and we sometimes see things differently. Recently Sweet Maria texted me upstairs at breakfast. She said there were "creeps" waiting for me in the kitchen. I was guessing "crepes" but had my fingers crossed. When I got to the kitchen to see who was there, Maria was looking at the weather forecast. The exchange went something like this:

> Maria (shaking her head): "It's going to rain today."
> Me (bright-eyed and smiling): "Isn't that terrific? Sounds cozy."
> Maria (grumbling under her breath): "Bob, just say something's bad, okay?"
> Maria (looking up after a short pause): "Did I just say that out loud?"

While different in so many ways, we both share a common faith and a strong sense of adventure. I find mine in traveling, talking with lots of people, and starting schools in war zones. Maria finds hers in the more difficult work of loving and nurturing our family, making places of peace in our lives, and giving us all a place to return to. Yet we've found our superpowers *because* of our differences, not *in spite* of them. We've used these differences to sort out what things are worth the effort to pursue and which ones we should leave behind.

Our kids and the people they love are my teachers, my advisors, and the ones I go to for clarity on the many things I don't quite understand. They help me sort into piles those things that will last in my life and the others that won't. As you embark on this journey to identify your ambitions, find these kinds of people to surround yourself with. It'll be worth the effort.

Someone wiser than me once asked, "If God answered every one of your prayers, would it change anybody's life except your own?" I've seen Maria's prayers change countless lives. I know her prayer for you and for me would be that we would leave all the planning behind, figure out what our lasting ambitions are, and get back to building those rocket ships that were supposed to be our lives. To do this, she would want us to trade what is easily available for what is actually worthwhile. It's a distinction that has the power to change everything in your life.

Chapter 2

THERMOMETER

We all are going to mess up.

When I was in kindergarten, we had nap time. We would all curl up on mats on the floor after an hour or two of loosely paying attention. I think there's a strong argument out there that we should continue this at all ages and stages of our lives. The big honor in class was to be the "wake-up fairy." This person would don a set of gender-neutral fairy wings and, with wand in hand, tap each of the sleeping students when it was time to wake up. This was one of my first ambitions I can recall. I wanted those wings. I wanted that wand. I wanted them badly. I wanted to be able to wield that kind of power over others. Think back. What was your earliest ambition? How long was it before you got your shot at it? And when you did get your shot, what did you do with it?

After weeks of impatiently waiting and practicing in front of the mirror at home, my day came. I strapped on the wings, grabbed the wand, and ran across the classroom to wake up my best friend. Unfortunately, in my fairy-induced exuberance to get to my friend, I tripped over a sleeping classmate's nose and broke it. It turns out this was a large enough infraction to have me immediately lose my wake-up fairy duties. Like Icarus, I had flown too close to the sun and it cost me my wings. My ambition became my undoing.

Failure happens. I should have made a bumper sticker or a hoodie. You know this is true because it's happened to you before, and it'll happen to you again. You swing for the fences, your fairy wish is granted, you run with joy and anticipation, and the wheels come completely off. This is the way ambitions work—sometimes they simply don't. Resist the tendency to be discouraged or thrown off the scent when it happens to you. It's what you do next that says a lot about who you are.

⁓

I was a good kid in junior high school but a confused one. My dad smoked cigarettes when I was growing up, so I figured I would too. Back then, cigarettes were sold at the post office in a vending machine. You could pick up a roll of stamps and emphysema on the same trip. After school one day, I went to the post office to get a Marlboro hard pack for myself. The soft pack was for novices, but the Marlboro hard pack had a lid and everything, so it made you look James Dean cool. It cost only two quarters for a pack because tobacco companies hadn't been sued for billions and people didn't know they would die if they smoked. Even the Marlboro Man didn't know back then.

Just after I put my second quarter in and pulled the lever, my Boy Scout leader came up behind me. It was certainly an awkward moment. I wanted to say that the cigarettes were for my mom, but the scoutmaster knew my mom and that she didn't smoke. So I did the honorable thing and told him they were for my sister.

Some of us start early telling lies about ourselves or others. We do this for a number of reasons, but primarily because we're uncertain about who we are and how we fit into the larger arc of our lives. We're insecure and looking for acceptance, so we do dumb things in our desperation. We smoke or cuss or dress or act like someone we really aren't to gain acceptance from people we don't really know. We're all going to make mistakes. Some are premeditated and weirdly intended to be self-destructive. Others just arise simply because we don't understand what is happening around us. Those are the mistakes that remind us of our humanity and help us be truthful with ourselves about the fact that we don't have it all figured out. I'll give you an example.

I'm usually a pretty healthy, upbeat guy. For me the glass is not just half-full but overflowing-so-get-a-bigger-one. But when I get sick, the wheels totally fall off. I get sad and melancholy and weak. It's beyond silly. It's almost clinical. I catch a simple cold and I act like I'm on chemo. What makes things worse is my need to constantly check to see which way I'm going. *Is that a new ache? Am I getting better or sicker? Will I even make it? How about now? Better or sicker? Have I updated my will? Better or sicker?* I open the refrigerator door and think I'm walking toward the light.

One time when our children were young, I caught the flu. It would've been no big deal for anyone else, but this is me, so I assumed it was terminal. This angel-of-death flu started to come on really strong as we all went to bed one night. I wanted to keep track of my demise as I slipped toward the abyss (and also milk this thing for as much sympathy as I could get from Sweet Maria). I gave her updates every few minutes on how truly awful I felt. I thought an update every three to five minutes would be just about right. In the middle of the night, I was feeling worse than I could describe, so I thought I should get some additional proof of how much I was suffering. I went to the bathroom where we kept our medicines to find a thermometer in the cabinet.

After rummaging through mostly empty medicine bottles and baby supplies collected over the years, I found a thermometer and put it under my tongue. I planned to show Maria my triple-digit temperature so she'd know how heroic I was to still be clinging to life. My mom always told me as a kid how I needed to get the thermometer way under my tongue, or the reading wouldn't be accurate. I buried it as far as it would go.

I took the thermometer out of my mouth a couple of times to see how high it was reading. I really couldn't tell. But that didn't surprise me because I probably didn't have long to live. I put it back under my tongue for a couple more minutes and checked again, imagining there was hardly enough mercury in the thermometer to record how high my temperature was. It was dark and I couldn't quite make out the numbers, so I woke up Maria and asked for help. As I slowly pulled the thermometer out of my mouth to give to her, I said, "Hey, why is there a big knob at the end of this thermometer?" Maria looked back at me for a long moment and then was swept over with laugher and horror.

She broke the news to me that the bulb was to prevent the thermometer from going missing when it gets used. "Go missing?" I was processing the information slowly as I pulled the thermometer from my mouth. I had grabbed the kids' rectal thermometer by mistake.

∽

I used to think that we had to have our act together for God to use us and for our ambitions to be attainable, but I don't think that anymore. Here's the incredible thing: I couldn't even take my own temperature, but God still finds a way to use me. He'll use you, too, if you're willing. Something happens when we mess up. We get to start fresh. Are we going to get it wrong from time to time? Yep. Will we make big things out of small things? You bet. Yet God is infinitely patient with us. Sometimes the mistakes are small ones and sometimes they're big ones. I'm still messing up the simple things in my life like taking my temperature, but God calls me His own nonetheless. He does the same with you. We need to get this straight as we explore our ambitions, or we'll let our past failures block our bright futures.

We've all suffered setbacks. Maybe you've tried to go after some audacious dreams that got derailed along the way. Maybe a few others sunk at the dock. What do you do when this happens? This book isn't full of airtight answers, but it will ask a few questions and offer a pathway to reframe your thinking. In the meantime, though, don't feel bad about not being perfect before you start.

Chapter 3

GET UNDER THE ICE CAP

Keep asking the important questions.

There's a city in the high desert in California called "Goffs." I'm not kidding. It's one of those towns typical of the West, a bustling little community that disappeared when they built a bigger, better highway diverting traffic somewhere else. It came up for sale recently, so I offered $7,500 cash for the whole town if they threw in both street signs. I'm waiting for an answer, but so far it's been crickets (which are the only things living in the town). I've already decided if I get the place, I'm going elect myself the mayor. I'll hold big rallies and have a parade. I'll have bumper stickers made and probably shoot off some bottle rockets. Sweet Maria said she isn't coming, so I'll be the only person voting. It should be a landslide if it rains hard enough, and there will be no hanging chads, unless a guy named Chad shows up and starts hanging out.

Once I take over as mayor of Goffs, I'm going to make all the rules. Speeding won't just be allowed; it will be encouraged if you're moving toward something that matters. There will be no stopping at stop signs, because I'm taking them down if they keep people from moving toward their beautiful, lasting ambitions. People will be allowed to yield to traffic but not to difficulties. There will always be reconstruction work, though. Some of our ideas and perceptions will be tear-downs, while others will just need some major remodeling when it comes to limiting beliefs. The town will be filled with people full of the guts and grit it takes to dig deep and get at the foundations of what they believe and why they believe it. There will be signs and hard hats and Big Gulp cups and successes and failures everywhere. These aren't scorecards; they are simply evidence that people are hard at work.

I once owned an old Victorian home that needed a lot of repairs. When I purchased it, I did a little research, and it turns out it was once owned by Wyatt Earp. How cool is that? He had evidently moved to San Diego after the whole OK Corral thing. The problem with the house wasn't its age; the problem was with its accessibility. You see, the only way you could get inside was by climbing a lot of steps. This meant that only some people could get in. Only the ones without problems and limitations. We wanted everybody to have access to this place, so I replaced all these steps with ramps so everyone who wanted to get in, could. This book is not about taking a series of steps; it's about on-ramping your ambitions. I want everybody to get in. I want *you* to get in—but only if you want to.

Here's a tip. Don't make the things in this book too simple or too complex. I'm aiming for somewhere in between—which is the place where most of us are. You can insert your name here for the kind of place you want to build, but for me, it's a place called Goffs.

Who are you? Where are you? What do you want?

I've been flying airplanes for twenty years. Still, every time I come in for a landing, I tell the tower I'm a student pilot. Mainly because I still am. What I've found is the people in the control tower are nicer to me over the radio because I'm a student. No one cuts off a student driver, right? Well, some of you do, but you should feel really bad about it. If you want to engage your ambitions like you never have before, self-identify as a student in all things—be a student dater, student husband, student employee. You get the idea. We're all amateurs at love and acceptance. Nobody goes pro and gets sponsored by Hershey's Kisses or the Hallmark Channel. Don't be a pain, but ask people you admire lots of questions. Let them know you're still a student and want to learn. Sure, some people will blow you off, but don't sweat it. They're just insecure or distracted. Most people will want to help you out and the kind ones always will.

Don't act like you've got it all figured out. Nobody wants to give that person extra time. Instead, be humble, self-aware, and punishingly truthful. Jesus never had a problem with people who knew their shortcomings; He didn't tolerate rookies who pretended to have gone All-Pro and have it all figured out but were just faking it. Once we get real with where we actually are and our desperate need for God's help, He's got a person He can do something with, and He'll drop the people you'll need in your path to help. Your job is to find them.

Being a pilot comes in handy because our family lives for part of each year in the Lodge we built in a remote location in British Columbia, Canada, and I fly a seaplane in and out. I love everything about flying except talking on the radio to air traffic controllers. Normally I like to talk to people, probably to a fault, but getting on the radio in the airplane to talk with a control tower has always intimidated me. They talk so fast and expect you to know what they're saying. I might be wrong, but I think I heard a controller ordering a pizza once. I'm also afraid I'll say the wrong thing on the radio and end up redirected to Saskatchewan, so I don't say anything, which can also get me in trouble.

I decided maybe the problem was that I'd never met a controller in a tower, so I called the local airport and made an appointment to meet one. I got to the flight control center, walked up several flights of stairs, and stepped into what looked like a movie set. There were several people sitting in front of screens. Each screen had dozens of dots representing airplanes with actual people in them. The controllers spoke infrequently to each pilot, but when they did, they didn't try to give them all the instructions they could possibly give. Each of the controllers was in charge of just a few dots, and their goals were simple. They wanted to help each plane get to its destination and avoid hitting other ones along the way.

Up in the tower, one of the controllers took me aside and said, "Bob, I know it's hard to talk on the radio sometimes, and it can feel confusing and more than a little intimidating. Everyone feels this way sometimes. So just do this: Say who you are, where you are, and what you want. Then listen closely." A lot of people feel the same way about talking to God or discovering their ambitions that I felt about talking to the control tower. They're up in the air, don't want to crash or hit someone else, and just need a little help getting to their destination.

Make no mistake, identifying and pursuing your ambitions is going to take a lot of courage and clarity. It's also going to take more than a little personal reflection. Organizing your thoughts around these three questions will help you accomplish in the future what you haven't been able to make happen in the past.

Start with acknowledging that deeper longing within you. If I had to take a guess, that's why you're here. You can feel it. I don't even have to define what *it* is—you know exactly what I'm talking about. *It* is that "something more to life" rumbling around in your gut, that tug drawing you toward a scary, audacious dream. It nags you when you feel stuck at a job you once wanted but have since outgrown. It fuels the late-night conversations before college graduation. It hovers around coffee shops and kitchen tables when parents become empty nesters. It is everywhere. Boardrooms and bedrooms, subways and surf shops, galleys and galleries. It is in the passenger seat on a long road trip, uttered through quiet prayers, and found in pop song lyrics. These are all expressions of us searching for a life that matters.

I believe this pursuit is a combination of finding answers to the three big questions: Who are you? Where are you? What do you want? These are some simple words, but they are actually some of the most beautiful, most difficult, and most confusing questions we can ask of ourselves. They can be a cocktail of identity, desire, purpose, rejection, life experience, struggle, fear, hope, and longing rolled into one. If we're going to discover and realize our most beautiful and lasting ambitions—the ones that are really worth pursuing—we have to lean into these questions.

By the way, I've never met anyone who had all of this figured out—even if they told me they did. In fact, if they said they did, I'd take it as proof they needed to keep searching. Maybe this side of heaven life was made for searching. Instead of a final destination, or striving for complete certainty, maybe our ambitions are like the smell of a pie in the oven—a reminder and invitation to follow the scent, to enter, to keep trying, keep looking, and keep discovering.

Maybe you know your ambitions (or have a pretty good sense of them) but have been too afraid to make any moves. There are a lot of people in this exact spot. Perhaps you've been living with unexecuted dreams for years, wearing them like an old T-shirt, yet avoiding them like a weird roommate. This is something that happens to our best ideas all the time. We're so close to them, or we've ignored them for so long, that we can't even see them for what they are anymore. Then just when we think we have corralled them, they change. When this happens, don't get bummed out; get current with your new ambitions. I know it feels like a hassle, but it's a good thing. We're supposed to be new creations, and there will be nothing new about us if everything remains the same.

I get it—all of it. That's why I wrote this book. To help you get unstuck. I want you to line up all your ambitions and distinguish between the ones that sound good but aren't, the ones you should completely ignore, and the ones that are worth throwing everything you've got into. When you figure these things out, in Starbucks parlance, I don't want you to merely go Tall or Grande; I want you to go Venti on them.

What I'm offering is a path, not a prescription. It's a path I've tried to take my whole life. The truth is, I'm still cutting trail myself, but it's a path I've seen thousands of others take as well. I think it works pretty well, but hear me clearly about this: doing what I suggest in these pages won't fix all your problems. It won't fill in your bald spots, get you to fit into skinny jeans, give you the dimples you wish you had, or make you a gazillionaire. What it will do, though, if you're willing to put in the work, is lead you to the life you're longing for. A life of purpose, full to the brim with intention and anticipation. A life lived with your eyes wide open, where you actually want what you see ahead of you rather than obsessing over the past or living scared about the future. A life that leads to purpose and legacy and fulfillment. It's the life you have been too confused or afraid or discouraged or disillusioned to move toward. It's a life where you can sort out what's worth your time and what isn't.

Can we just look each other in the eye through these pages and say, *No more doing what merely occupies, entertains, and numbs us?* It's time to go after your dreams, your faith, and your ambitions with gusto. It's just simply time. You know it. I know it. The people who love us know it. Let's stop deferring, ignoring, and screwing around, distracting ourselves with things that won't really matter next week, much less in our next life. Let's instead throw our efforts and emotional weight into those ambitions which will outlast us and leave all the rest behind.

In this journey we're setting out on, I'm not your guide; I'm a Sherpa. I'll tell you why. Guides tell someone what mountain to climb. They order all the equipment, get the food, buy the tents, and tell the climber what route to take and direct all of the steps taken. Sherpas, on the other hand, let the climber pick the mountain to be climbed, then spend most of their time laying the ropes in advance so the climber can move a little faster. More importantly, Sherpas tell climbers what they *don't* need to take in order to make the summit. If you've ever seen an overeager climber, you know exactly what I'm talking about. Their pack is so loaded down with things they don't really need that they'll never go the distance or get to the destination. The same is true for you, and we're going to need to offload quite a bit of what we've accumulated if we're going to make it to the top of our ambitions.

Tie your boot laces, get your backpack on, and let's go.

Chapter 4

WHO ARE YOU?

We can't fix what we don't understand.

A few years ago, someone I loved had a stroke. This is a cruel medical problem because often, in addition to causing physical limitations, it robs its victims of some of what they cherish the most—their memories. The doctor explained how the brain attempts to knit itself back together and recreate the pathways and circuitry disrupted by the stroke. The doctor recommended photographs be up on the walls of the hospital room to help jog her memory as her brain reconnected with itself. She would stare long and hard at the walls and point. One by one, she figured out the photographs. "That's my husband. That's my daughter. This one is our dog." It took a while, but eventually she figured out every photograph—except one. It was a photograph of her.

It's easy to think we've got everyone else figured out. But what about ourselves? Maybe you're starting this process of identifying and chasing your dreams and realize you've been looking at everyone else without ever really seeing yourself. Perhaps there have been so many big changes in your life that you feel estranged from the person you once knew so well; you don't recognize yourself anymore. Listen up. Don't ignore this; get real with it.

Did the person you used to adore get buried in the responsibilities of growing a career, folding laundry, or waiting in the school pickup line? Is your past shouting so loud you can't hear the future calling your name? Have you spent so much time and energy trying to meet others' expectations of you that you forgot what you really want for yourself? Or maybe you've never taken the time and space you need to meet your real self for the first time.

Making this introduction to yourself can be hard and sometimes even a little scary. Don't let that head-fake you. Don't defer starting, and don't quit trying. It's necessary work if you want to move forward with your ambitions. Here's why: there is massive power in self-awareness. Don't overlook or underestimate it. It's not indulgent to spend some time reflecting on your life; in fact, it's foolish not to. If you need a counselor to help you get at what's under the hood in your life, get two. If you need a break from your job, take one. You've got to figure out who you are before you can decide who you're going to be. Only then will you be able to sort out whether what you want is worth the time and sacrifice it will take to get it.

I have a friend with a shirt that says "I'm more confused than a chameleon in a bag of Skittles." Trying to be who everyone thinks or expects us to be can be exhausting. Start getting out of that mess by making it known to yourself and those around you that you're not going to let others decide who you are anymore. It's God alone who names you—and here is some great news—you are simply His.

Don't get me wrong. I'm not saying you should make this journey all about you. If you do, your life and your world will get really small in a hurry. What I *am* saying is that discovering who you *really* are and what really makes you tick is worth the effort. It is the good, hard work of being alive. Show up for that. Do it today, not next week or "someday." Do it right now. We only have the blink of an eye to figure our lives out. Don't waste any more years waiting for an easier time to come, because it won't.

⁀

One day at the Lodge we built in Canada, a helicopter landed on our lawn. We don't get many visitors because we live so remotely, so I wondered if there had been a mechanical problem. A man jumped out of the helicopter, ran up to me, and gave me a kiss on each cheek. "My name is Deni and I'm a Frenchman," he said. *Evidently,* I thought to myself.

Deni said he had been flying in the nearby mountains and found a huge ice cave he wanted to show me. I've lived up the inlet for twenty-five years and know the place pretty well. I told Deni I doubted there was a cave I didn't know about. Four minutes later, my new friend and I were in the air heading for the glaciers. Like my son Rich once said when he threw a bullet he found into our campfire to see what would happen, what could possibly go wrong?

We landed and Deni led me to a small opening in the glacier. He nodded his head toward the hole a couple of times as if saying, *This is it.* After sizing up the small hole, I glanced down at my midsection to make sure my circumference could fit. Standing on a glacier with this new friend, I realized climbing underneath a glacier through a small opening seemed like a really bad idea. So, naturally, I was eager to get started. After we made our way past the opening, the path eventually opened up enough to hunch over, and then a bit more to walk through. Sure enough, underneath a hundred-foot layer of blue ice cap, there was a huge cave extending farther than I could see.

Why am I telling you this? Because it's a great image for you and for me. Most of the things that drive us—big and small—usually have a place of origin far below the surface. You may not even know about these places or have taken the time to explore them. Answering the question *Who are you?* requires we stop entertaining ourselves building snowmen on the surface and get under the ice cap. That's the only way to figure out what's really going on underneath our actions.

If we can learn what the core motivations behind our actions are, we can figure out where they came from and take the action necessary to make progress forward. Not a course around them but through them. It can sometimes be weird and ambiguous work to access our big ideas, and headway is often made through small openings. Yet this work is absolutely necessary if we want to make some bold moves toward those few ambitions that will be worth the effort to accomplish.

If we don't take the time to discover what's beneath the surface in relationships, or faith, or careers, we won't go for what's best; we'll just keep reaching for whatever is available and easily accessible. Going under the ice cap requires asking ourselves *Why did I do that?* Make a time and a place to do this. If you needed dialysis, you wouldn't miss the appointment because a meeting came up. Trust me, you need this uninterrupted time. Do whatever it takes to get it.

I have a friend who has taken this suggestion of mine so seriously she *actually* goes to the parking lot outside of a dialysis center each week, parks the car, and spends time reflecting on those things underneath her life that are driving the things on the surface. She treats this time like an appointment she can't miss because she recognizes that how she lives her life depends upon it.

An unexpectant life is one that is merely on repeat. A life lived in constant anticipation, on the other hand, is one willing to do a load of self-examination. We can't fix what we won't take the time to understand. If you're willing to make the trip under the surface, you'll find some pretty great stuff there. Some hard stuff? Sure. Some scary stuff? You bet. Some stuff you'd rather avoid? Definitely. But at least you'll understand the *real* you. You'll be dealing with the real causes of your insecurity, not merely the manifestations of it. You'll confront the actual impediments in your life, not just the perceived ones. Why settle for the surface-level version of yourself when you can go a little deeper and discover the core of who you really are? Don't waste another moment without getting to know yourself. You're worth it. Don't believe this simply because I say so, but because God does.

Chapter 5

WHERE ARE YOU?

It takes courage to get honest
about your location.

D id you know we're hurtling through space, around the sun, at twenty-five thousand miles an hour? The earth is also spinning at over one thousand miles an hour on its axis. Your brain can process what your eyes see right now in thirteen milliseconds. If you ever thought you were moving too slowly or weren't getting much done, you were wrong. If you have ever called yourself a couch potato, think again. I don't care who you are; you're making moves. We all are.

I have a silly game I play with myself a dozen times a day when I walk into various rooms. I try to figure out where north is. Try it now: count to three, then point your arm in the direction where you think true north is. Even if you're in an elevator or a waiting room, in a classroom, just got pulled over by a cop, or are in the dentist chair. Ready? Go. I carry a compass with me in my pocket, but you can check the compass on your phone and see how far off you were. Here's the point: nobody has it all figured out. With the speed we're moving, it's easy to get a little turned around and a couple of degrees off.

This tees up the next question I have for you: *Where are you?*

At first glance, this one seems a little easier to answer. We're in the line at McDonald's, stuck in traffic, cramming for a final, itching for a promotion, stuck in a relationship, reading a book. Here's what I want you to do. Instead of thinking geography, I want you to think biography. Figuring out *where* you really are is a big part of discovering *who* you really are right now.

> Are you in a job that's sucking you bone dry, but you don't know how you'll pay rent or the mortgage without it? That's where you are.
>
> Are you in a toxic relationship but are so exhausted or have grown so codependent that you stay? That's where you are.
>
> Is your mind being blown by how blessed you are with your spouse or your friendships or your community? That's where you are.
>
> Are you still believing you don't have what it takes to achieve your big vision? That's where you are.
>
> Are you fuming over a wrong done to you or a relationship that got wonky? That's where you are.

Life can be delightfully wonderful, and it can also be punishingly difficult. I won't keep it a secret for the end of the book. If you want to fast-track your ambitions, get real about where you are right now. If you want to get in the race, you need a starting line. The only way you can establish the beginning of your journey is with brutal honesty. If you're in a huge situational crack, acknowledge it. Call it what it is. It stinks. It's unfair. It's dumbfounding. If you feel like you need to, scream into your pillow or punch a wall—just figure out why. (Actually, don't punch the wall. You'll just freak everyone out, break your hand, and need to replace a lot of drywall. Get a counselor; it'll work out better for everyone.)

Even if you're a positivity junkie like me, don't feel like you're disappointing God by being honest about how low you feel. Your honesty isn't letting people down; you're letting God in. Be wise enough to stay optimistic while you're getting clear on where you are in your life. Meanwhile, become more situationally aware of what's going on within and around you. In other words, figure out where you are.

The question *Where are you?* is one of the first interactions we see in the Bible between God and the people like us that He made. When it got weird, Adam and Eve forgot who they were and hid. When God asked, *Where are you?*, He wasn't looking for a literal answer, of course. God knows everything, even if we don't understand or won't acknowledge it. He wasn't talking about longitude and latitude; He was addressing their state of mind. He wanted to know whether *they* knew where they were. They were tucked in a bush, yes, but they were really in a place called shame. Don't get punked by your past. It will lie to you, distract you, try to get your attention, and then laugh at you for looking. Shame has one goal and one goal alone: to keep you cemented in a dark past while it hides a beautiful future from you.

Every single person is somewhere. I know that seems like an obvious statement, and it is in one respect. But how many people really know where they are in their lives? Figuring it out is where it gets real. The ironic thing is that most of us already know the deeper answer, but we're afraid to say it out loud. *I'm in my addiction. I'm coasting in my marriage. I'm selling myself short and taking the easy route. I'm afraid I'll be discovered.* For me the answer often is, *I'm going so fast and doing so much I'm missing the more important things I could be sharing with my friends and family.*

So, here's your moment. Where are you? Be courageous. Figure it out, own it, then write it down or say it out loud. Have a friend take you to Starbucks, make them pay, and have three minutes of authenticity together. Tell someone, perhaps even a few people you trust, where you really are. If you can't find the words, slip them the note you wrote. We need to tell people where we really are so they can meet us there. Tell God, too, and for Pete's sake, shoot straight. Don't green screen your life or airbrush your circumstances to make them look different than what's really happening. God already knows—He's been waiting in the garden and wants you to get honest enough with yourself and with Him to just say it. Besides, He likes to hear the sound of your voice. Use it and tell Him. Once we figure out where we are, He can lead us from there.

One last thing. Don't let this kind of honesty discourage you. It's okay to be somewhere and wish you were in a different spot. It happens to me all the time. It's where I am right now. It's where I was yesterday. But it's not where I'm planning to be tomorrow. In short, I'm not camping out in my uncertainty; I'm figuring it out with God.

What are you waiting for? Let's do this thing. We're all along for different versions of the same ride, so you'll have lots of company. We'll sit close, and when we arrive, it'll look like a clown car as we all start getting out.

We can't get on the path toward our ambitions without figuring out where we are. What has felt like your resting place is now a starting line. If you have the honesty and guts for it, what you've been stuck in is what you'll be freed from. Where you are today is simply the harbor from which your ship is about to sail. Cut loose the lines. The horizon is where you're heading because it's where your ambitions reside.

Chapter 6

WHAT DO YOU WANT?

Trade what is simply available
for what will truly last.

When I was in junior high school, I went with my parents to Hawaii. I was immediately smitten. Blue skies, crystal-clear water, white sand beaches, chocolate-covered macadamia nuts, and shaved ice with rainbow-colored syrup. My ambition at thirteen years old was to some-day get a small place on the water in Hawaii. It seemed doable enough, right? I mean, how many puka shells could a beach house cost anyway? When I grew up, sadly, I found out how much a small place on the water in Hawaii costs: slightly more than a ship full of hundred-dollar bills.

Our dreams are birthed in childlike innocence, but as we grow up we discover more information that can be a buzzkill to our ambitions.

When I found out what a small place on the water actually cost, I wondered if I should abandon this dream. This is something we each decide at some point. We have an ambition and then face the headwinds that discouragement and reality and failure bring our way. That's when we need to decide if our ambition is still worth it.

It turns out millions of dollars will only get you a surf shack a block from the water in Hawaii. At the time, I didn't have ten bucks. You'll need to decide what you're going to do when you get some reality pushback on your dreams. If the front door is locked, you can walk away or look for a window that's ajar to crawl through. Some of your ambitions are going to take time or a little creativity to figure out. Don't quit on them. Wake up to new ways to get there, then do what it takes so you're ready when your time comes.

While a small home in the Hawaiian Islands will always be out of reach for me, a small boat wasn't. There aren't many marinas in Hawaii, and the few that are there don't have many slips. But get this—I found out that it was possible to rent a small boat slip for two hundred dollars a month if one became available. So I got on the waiting list at a marina in Honolulu. It's a pretty long list. I've been on it for over two decades now and guess what? I'm only two dead people from the top, and I'll have my small place on the water in Hawaii. Your ambitions are worth all the attention you're willing to give them. Be patient. Get creative. Give it some time. If you can't buy the house, get on the waiting list for the slip.

So, what do you want? I mean, what do you *really, really, really* want? Get it out there. It's not like you're removing your own appendix to say it; it's just not that hard to speak the words, and it will take less gauze. Get a starter list going. We'll revisit it later and build it out with more focus and intention. If you want a convertible Porsche, don't say you want world peace. Just get real about it. Wherever you are right now, just shout out as loudly as you can, "I want a Porsche!" You're not trying out for Miss America, and nobody is going to give you a crown and a bouquet of flowers for saying you want to end world hunger if you don't. Don't pretend to be noble. Be real and it will be the most noble thing you'll do all year. Trust me, heaven will be doing cartwheels if you will finally get real about what you really want.

In just a little bit, when we dive in further, you'll have a chance to get everything down into some kind of order. For now, start here. What do you want for your life? If you're like me, you want love, joy, happiness, meaning, purpose, and a more courageous faith. The trick to finding these things is discovering what ambitions you already have that will lead to them.

Guess what? For years you've already been quietly curating your life without knowing it. You know what works and what doesn't. What lights you up and what bums you out. What lasts and what disappears. We need to figure out what you've come up with so far so we can figure out what to do next. Trust what you've learned already; let it be your Sherpa.

Once again, the best engine to drive our ambitions is a strong sense of purpose. There's nothing really important about the vacation or the new pair of kicks or the convertible. These are things we might want for a time and might even enjoy for a while. They're the short game though. Don't confuse them with your ambitions. The long game is where your best ambitions reside. When you think you've found an ambition you want, figure out why you want it and whether you want it badly enough to do what it takes to get it.

We're all looking for meaning, but it's often lost behind a hedge of distractions, hurts, and disappointments. Figure out what these have been for you. Merely existing doesn't satisfy most of us, so we pursue inputs that ultimately distract us from our lack of direction. At some point, though, even the distractions aren't enough. Or someone else screws it up for us, and we end up wounded and lost again. The fix isn't easy, but it's this simple: We need to replace what we've settled for with what we've been longing for. We need to find ambitions worthy of our time and the effort it will take to pursue them.

For some, tremendous purpose will be found in a deeper expression of their faith. For others, it will be the accumulation of wealth or notoriety or adventure. Do whatever blows your hair back if you're playing the short game. If you're in it for the long haul and want to live a life steeped in purpose, a better long-term approach is to figure out who you want to be and let that inform what you do. Don't settle for what you're simply able to do; figure out what you were made to do, then do lots of that.

As we get into the process of identifying and working toward your ambitions, don't be too hard on yourself, okay? Going under the ice cap is hard work. It can get cold and lonely down there. Getting real is hard work too. If it were easy, you would have been there and back a dozen times already. Just ask Pinocchio. His ambition was to become less wooden and more real. It didn't happen overnight or without a couple of setbacks and a lot of wood shavings. Rather than lie about it and have your nose grow, get real and watch your faith explode.

A long time ago, a friend told me there's a difference between whittling and carving. One is just killing time, the other is laden with purpose. Keep carving. Engage the process; don't stifle it. Go ahead and want the corndog and the surfboard and the date to prom. There is absolutely nothing inherently wrong with wanting those things. Just be sure they're not the only ambitions you have. Take a look at what Jesus had on His list of ambitions and lift a few onto yours. His list wasn't very long, but it changed the world forever. He was a master at choosing ambitions that were worth it.

Get this. His ambition was you. It was everyone else He created too. He made us with eternity in mind, sure, but also for tomorrow and the next day and the next, filled with touching lives with incredible intentionality. Identify what has captured your attention and what has distracted you. Fill your days with dozens of small, intentional acts of love. Take note of those ambitions you already have that Jesus also demonstrated and move them higher on your list.

God made us to enjoy each other and to reflect Him, and He derives tremendous joy when He sees us pursuing our unique desires with the skill sets He put in our individual tool boxes. I'm not really sure where He stands on corndogs, but I know He's inviting us into lives that are more expansive and expressive, more loving and unselfish. He wants us to reflect His character in what we want and have these desires dwarf anything else that gets in the way. I'm certain He's not asking you to mimic someone else's ideas, desires, and dreams. Sure, be inspired by the lives other people are living and riff on them if it helps you get clarity, but as Sweet Maria tells me all the time (and as we'll discuss later), keep your eyes on your own paper.

So, let me ask you again. What do you want? Jesus asked people what they wanted all the time. He didn't have problems with the people who messed up grappling with the issues in their lives; He didn't like it when people faked it. If you find yourself tempted to be artificial or disingenuous, find a new way to deal with your insecurity. Bite your tongue, swallow a goldfish, or shave off your eyebrows if you need to, but break the cycle. Look at Jesus. He surrounded Himself with disciples who couldn't get the nets on the right side of the boat most of the time. At times they had desires that must have seemed superficial at best. But Jesus was kind, direct, and never mean to them. When you're real and authentic with Him, He won't beat you up when you mess up because He's embarrassed by you; He'll embrace you because He loves you.

Remember the passage in the Bible where the blind man called out to Jesus so he could be healed? Jesus' friends tried to help out by telling the man to stop yelling, but the blind man just yelled even louder. Maybe you should do the same if people have been trying to get you to quiet down about your ambitions. Quit whispering them to yourself and, instead, start shouting them into the world. Jesus asked the blind guy the same question He asks all of us every day. "What do you want me to do for you?" The answer must have seemed pretty obvious to the blind guy. But just like God in the garden with Adam and Eve, I don't think Jesus needed to hear the answer. He wanted to make sure the blind guy was clear on his ambitions and knew what he wanted more than anything else. He wants the same thing from you too.

Where the story gets good is when the blind guy tells Jesus his deepest desire. "Rabbi, I want to see." I can imagine him saying this with pleading, outstretched arms. Jesus wants the same for you—to gain more clarity on your faith, relationships, and what He uniquely made you for. He wants you to really see. Quit merely asking for thicker glasses when Jesus has invited us to climb up on His shoulders for a better view.

Chapter 7

CHASE THE JEEP

There's a big difference between
waving at Jesus and following Him.

There I was, sitting at the kitchen table, little eight-year-old Bob. It had been a hard day of playing with my friends, riding our bikes through the streets of my neighborhood, playing make-believe down by the creek. There might've been a game or two of Wiffle ball, but I was never really good at that kind of thing. All this to say, I was famished as only a kid can be after a day of full-out kid stuff. So when I sat down at the table, I eagerly grabbed my fork and knife as I watched my mom bring plates across the kitchen, piled high with food I was about to pound. When the meal was set down, I went for it with reckless abandon.

That's when Mom furled her brow and said, "You're welcome," shaking her head.

"Oh, thank you. Sorry, Mom. I forgot."

This was not an uncommon moment for me growing up. I tended to miss my cues, and somehow this whole manners thing became a sticking point. "You're welcome" was always delivered with a wrinkled face intended to remind me, with a pinch of shame, that I'd messed up again and hadn't been polite. It's funny how these little things stick with you for a lifetime because, as I grew up, I always tried to beat people to the punch with my thank-yous so I wouldn't get an unwanted "you're welcome."

Before my first trip to Uganda, I read up on all the customs and practiced being polite in the mirror. Steeped in British traditions, Uganda is a place that is very formal and polite. Etiquette matters. Perhaps all the years of being hassled with reminders about good manners would pay off after all.

I got off the airplane in Entebbe and hadn't been on the ground for fifteen minutes when a Ugandan looked at me and said, "You're welcome." *Oh no, here we go again.* "Um, thank you," I replied. Five minutes later I apparently had messed up again and another Ugandan said, "You're welcome." *What the heck?* I thought to myself, a little frustrated. "Thank you," I stammered, wondering again about my offense. The third time a Ugandan said, "You're welcome," I was tempted to silently cuss to myself in Swahili, but I didn't know how to speak the language, and I don't cuss.

Then I realized something. I slowed their words down in my mind and understood they weren't doing what my mom and dad had done through the years. They were actually saying, "You are welcome." As in, *you are welcome here.* These weren't words of correction; they were words of invitation. As a quick aside, here's a tip worth remembering if you want to achieve your ambitions. Don't be so eager to correct people; welcome them instead. Accept them. Love them without any angle or agenda. Start with yourself.

After recalibrating all the words of welcome I had received, I joined up with some colleagues, and we got in a Jeep and drove to a village not far from the airport. On my first trip to Uganda, I wanted to meet some Ugandan kids, kick a soccer ball around with them, and hear about their hopes. We got to the village, and the kids did not disappoint. Despite the hardships they had faced in their war-torn country, they were full of optimism and bubbling over with laughter, bright eyes, and contagious smiles. But they were in tremendous need. I knew I was on the trail of something lasting. Turns out this trip was the start of a twenty-five-year ambition to help out in Uganda. Even after all this time, I'm still learning.

After an afternoon playing with the kids and realizing a new dream was growing in my heart, we got back in the Jeep. I was waving goodbye and about ten kids started running behind the Jeep as we pulled away. I kept waving, all of us smiling and laughing, and the pack of running kids started to grow. Now there were twenty of them running after us. I figured one waving hand wasn't enough for them, so I got both hands going, waving as fast as I could. Now there were thirty kids. I'm a big fan of waving, and I hate goodbyes, but after several minutes of this my arms started to get tired. I asked the driver what the deal was as the crowd of kids now running after the car had grown to forty. He told me with a grin that the gesture of waving your hand in North America is used to say hi or goodbye. In Uganda it means "follow me."

What I realized in that moment is this is exactly what I've been doing to Jesus for most of my life. It's what I've done with my ambitions too. I've been merely waving at what I've been invited to follow.

When Jesus invited you on this adventure called your life, He did it so you could fulfill the ambitions He has for you—to be fully alive and fully His. He also wants you to align your faith with your talents and chase after the Jeep. He wants you to stare down your fears knowing He's got your back and can handle anything that comes your way. It's not as simple as this though. Oftentimes we compartmentalize our faith—it's what we do in church or during a daily devotion we feel guilty for skipping.

On this path to discovering and living your most beautiful, lasting ambitions, you're going to have to activate your faith in order to drive your life. You're going to have to give it all to Him. Jesus is knocking on the door of your life because He wants the whole room, not to just have you take a safe look at Him through a peephole or the crack between the door and the crack you're in.

⁓

I was traveling in the Midwest and arrived at my hotel a little after one o'clock in the morning. It had been a long day, and I was barely able to stay awake. I think the hotel attendant was in the same boat, because it took him forever to retrieve my reservation and finally give me my room key. I curled up in a lobby armchair while I waited—maybe I could squeeze in a few z's.

When I finally got my key and made it to the door of my room, I slipped inside and threw my bag on the bed. I fumbled around for the light switches, flipped on the lights, and, to my absolute shock, discovered there was a woman in the room. She started screaming, "This is my room!" I looked at my key and said, "This is my room!" as I backed up toward the door. I grabbed my bag and ran out of the room as fast as I could. I felt like Joseph.

Suffice it to say I was wide awake by then and pretty miffed at the mistake the guy at the counter had made. I tried to control my frustration as I walked back to the desk, tossed the card key back at him, and asked if I could have a room that didn't already have a person sleeping in my bed. The guy looked up with glazed eyes, said, "Dude, sorry man," slipped me a new card key, and went back to the game he was playing on his phone. Feeling less than reassured, I got to my second room of the early morning and thankfully had the room all to myself.

These days, I'm a little more tentative whenever I walk into a hotel room. I'm sure you will be now too. I'm tempted to throw a flashbang grenade in first and yell something like "Fire in the hole!" before entering. Our experiences, both good and bad, shape us or scar us.

Here's the point. As I've reflected on my ambitions, there have been countless times when I've told myself I've given Jesus the whole room, when what I've actually done is just emptied a couple of drawers or cleared off several inches of space in the closet for Him to hang a few ideas in my life. The simple but difficult fact is, He wants the whole room and everything in it—including us. Many of us live like hoarders, though, and there's not a lot of space left to give to Jesus even if we wanted to. We won't be able to advance our worthwhile ambitions if our lives are already fully occupied.

Think for a moment what you've filled your room with, both good and bad. Activities like careers or bowling or fly fishing. Attitudes you've experienced, like worry, anger, frustration, joy, or empathy. Some of these things are good and beautiful and lasting. Others are trespassers in your life. Jesus isn't going to be satisfied standing outside your door knocking while you try to tidy up before letting Him in. God doesn't want us to invite Him to sit quietly in a corner like a celebrity guest either. He's not our concierge or our butler, our muse or our roommate. Jesus is a King who came to make a kingdom, but He's not going to try to build it on top of our stuff or around all of our activities. If the room is full, we can invite Him in all we want, but we should expect that He's more likely to do major renovations than just rearrange the furniture or provide us room service. If the room is already full, He'll just wait to come more fully into our lives when it isn't.

Jesus didn't say He'd know the room was His if we said a moonlit prayer at camp or if we told everybody it was His room or if we used all the right words or showed up at church on Sundays or did a bunch of nice things for Him. Jesus said people would know whose room it is by what happens both inside and outside of it. Simply put, He's more likely to put much of what you've collected in a dumpster and light it on fire than turn down your bed and put a mint on your pillow. There's no do-not-disturb sign we can hang on the door. If you fill your life with Jesus and operate with love and grace, you'll be in the right place. If you express your faith through your love, you're doing it correctly. If you trust in Him, you'll get the rest you need.

Sometimes we make following Jesus a lot more complicated than Jesus instructed. The fix is a simpler, more intentional faith, not a busier or easier one. Complicated theology isn't bad; Jesus just never said it was a prerequisite or qualification for the unschooled, ordinary people He invited to follow Him. Certainly learn a ton about what you believe, but don't be like the self-identified "teachers" who gave educated waves to Him. You don't need a bunch of twenty-dollar words to couple your faith to your ambitions. When your faith is anchored by the few things God said we should care about, it will be more than enough to keep you clear and focused on the road ahead.

Let's say you clear the room of everything in your faith and ask yourself, "If I had to add one thing back to my life, what would it be?" It sounds like one of those moments when you think you're supposed to give a Sunday school answer and say, "Jesus?" That's usually a safe bet, but not always the most honest answer. But here, if I cleared the room of absolutely everything else, the first thing I *would* add back to my life is Jesus. Not all the trappings and manufactured religious rules and arguments that aren't things Jesus spent His time on. In fact, I'd lose all the religious talk and complicated words that create distance between people rather than provide clarity and unity among them.

The second thing I'd add back to my life is a pretty easy pick as well. I'd add my family and friends. We won't travel far without the ones we've already traveled with. As you are pursuing your ambitions, don't miss out on, or mess up with, your family and friends. Your greatest rewards in life will be found in the handful of people you have developed beautiful, loving, authentic, vulnerable relationships with. When Jesus met the first disciples fishing, He told them to push out a little deeper. They thought it was a stupid idea, but you know what? They did it anyway. Push out into deeper waters with your relationships. I know it can be hard. Do it anyway. You'll find a kind of clarity about your ambitions in the deeper waters that you won't in the shallows.

The third thing I'd add would be the things that add joy, purpose, and fulfillment to my life. I'm not just talking about my vocation. For many of us, what we do for a career is how we make rent. It's honorable to have a job and provide for the ones you love. The problem is that some of us spend so much time trying to provide for our families that we're *not* providing for our families. What your family wants is you, not your earning potential. Get clear on the people, whimsy, and capers that have added the most meaning to your life and add these people and things back in. If you remember a time when you were engaged in meaningful, purposeful work and deeper, more authentic relationships but you no longer are, return to these things. Add them back to your life.

Here's a tougher question for most of us: what is the seventh or eighth or tenth thing you'd add back if you cleared the room of all the things you've collected in your life? Honestly, I'm not sure I even have room for a seventh thing. Isn't that crazy? It turns out I only have a few things that make up the most important parts of my life. I bet the same is true for you. Don't get distracted by people who insist on knowing your position on the thirteenth thing or something that isn't even on your radar at all. Keep your eye on the ball. Darkness doesn't need to destroy us; it only needs to distract us. If you want to get after your ambitions, don't take the bait.

Chapter 8

GETTING TO THE "NEW" PART

It doesn't matter who you were; God
cares about who you are becoming.

I didn't grow up in the Church, and while I speak at quite a few faith gatherings, one thing I've found to be true is that people don't grow where they are merely informed; they grow where they are fully accepted. Before we go any further, let me get this out on the table where we can talk about it. You are loved and accepted. One hundred percent. No qualifications. No prerequisites. You can't be good enough, smart enough, or nice enough to be loved by God. He decided He would love you before you decided you were interested in loving Him back. Even if God is no big deal for you, your life is a big deal to Him. You are some of His most creative work ever. Pursuing your ambitions needs to start from a position of acceptance, not compliance. Compliance only lasts until you decide you're not going to comply anymore. We won't be able to get to the best parts of our lives and faith without accessing the best parts of acceptance.

Like me, you are easy to love at times and not so much at others. Be honest—you know this is true. You are capable of being both a jerk and a relational genius, and you have immeasurable untapped potential. If you want to get to the worthwhile parts of your life, let's get some of the genius out of the bottle (and maybe leave a little more of the jerk inside). Sometimes it's easier to accept someone else than it is to accept yourself. The fix is easy. Give yourself a hug or two on this journey. Even if you're not a hugger, do it anyway. It's not going to make your hair fall out and it probably won't even leave marks. It's said that fish grow to the size of their bowls. If you've been stingy about giving and receiving love and acceptance, get a bigger bowl. You're going to need it.

You're probably doing a couple of things right and are a hot mess in other areas of your life. Me too. Accept it, but don't delight in it. Don't give your lesser angels the room and don't resign yourself to perpetually screwing up. You are in as much need of tremendous love and grace and kindness from God as we all are. Don't hoard what you're learning about these things either. Learn something new, and then get it in play. It's what we do with what we know that lets the world see who we really are.

Most of us have all the information we need, namely that God is love and He loves and accepts us completely. Have you messed up? Of course. What we need in order to launch forward with our ambitions is a clearer sense of what would be worth our time to pursue once we embrace an unreasonable amount of grace and acceptance. Along this journey, you're going to have to become a ninja at spotting anything in your way that is counter to God's love and is selling you a bill of goods that makes you question whether you're absolutely loved and accepted by Him.

෴

You might think that hate is the enemy of love. It's not. Hate is merely the opposite of love, but not its enemy. Hate only has as much power as we give it. Love works the same way. It's fear that stops love in its tracks every time. If you think about it for a moment, most of what we do is motivated by either love or fear. The trick is to figure out which one is doing the talking at any particular point in time. As we're figuring out our ambitions, we need to figure out what's been controlling our lives.

That can be confusing, though, because the voices behind these competing influences of reflection and reaction sound a lot like us. Because they *are* us. If we take the time to listen a little closer and with some discernment, we might find out that some of the ideas holding us back didn't actually originate with us. It was a parent or failed relationship or teacher or adversary who stole the microphone and is still doing the talking. We are all reflections of, or reactions to, the people who have been closest to us. It will take some work to ferret out the reasons underlying our inactions and hesitations, our irrational fears and our wise conclusions. If you want to get serious about finding or reactivating ambitions you've mothballed, this will require taking a purposeful pause from your usual activities to understand why you do what you do.

෴

I have a lot of immensely talented friends. They make movies, throw pottery, sing, and start organizations. They compete at the Olympics and lead governments or their agencies. They wash cars and mow lawns. Whether their passions are big or small in the world's eyes, all these people are uniquely gifted to excel at a few things with an unparalleled level of excellence. You have some of the same sets of abilities in you too. You might not be on television or walking the red carpet, but you have some areas in your life where you totally crush it. Maybe it's in your friendships or your job. Perhaps it's the way you love your neighbors across the street or across an ocean. You could be a great flautist or fisherman; it doesn't matter. What I'm getting at is this: God endowed each of us with something unique. The trick is to figure out what your thing is and how you're going to get it in play. Some people make careers out of these things, and a lot of people spend their whole lives trying to figure out what they are.

As we pursue our unexecuted ambitions, it's easy to let our capabilities decide who we'll be. Let me give you an example. I'm a lawyer and have been licensed to practice law in many states. I can pass a bar exam like some people pass a blood test. The only difference is that in the bar exam they just stick the needle in your head rather than your arm and for three days suck everything out of it. Just because I'm *capable* of being a lawyer, however, doesn't mean I was *made* to be a lawyer. Hear me when I say this—I don't think we should do what we're lousy at, but I also don't think we should let our capabilities, our careers, or our successes decide our future.

We're moving targets. You are not who you used to be, and thankfully I'm not either. Our desires and interests can and should change and be revised along the way. One of the people who wrote a letter in the Bible, Paul, said we're supposed to be *new creations* every day. If everything stays the same, we never get to the "new" part. New creations constantly find new opportunities and desires to pursue. If you're not finding new and bigger, more beautiful ambitions, you probably don't need to get smarter; you need to get newer. This means you will need to change a couple of things as you evolve. But you don't necessarily have to ditch the past altogether. Sometimes your capabilities will serve and point toward new ambitions. Let me explain.

There's an African proverb that says, "When two elephants fight, it is the grass that suffers." I grew up in a time of relative peace. Many people don't. I began learning of the suffering of young people in countries where conflicts were occurring. They were the grass being stomped on by some elephants in their warring nations.

After my first trip to Uganda, one of my ambitions was to start schools for children caught up in wars around the world. For more than twenty-five years, Uganda was locked in a civil war with the Lord's Resistance Army. We decided to start a school in Gulu, Uganda, which was ground zero for the war. At the time, the Lord's Resistance Army was still active in the area, and armed fighters on both sides of the conflict were everywhere. I was a trial lawyer at the time, and a pretty good one too. My team and I would win cases and began using the money we earned to build schools for kids in Uganda and, later, several other countries. I used what I already knew how to do to fund what I wanted to do. In short, I went with my strengths and found the opportunities that hadn't yet found me. Practicing law just became the way to do justice and pay for it. (Besides, if I baked brownies to raise money, I'm sure someone would have died.)

Having a day job and earning what I needed was a version of fundraising I could understand. Becoming a lawyer had been an ambition of mine when I was in my twenties, and it was something I was able to do well. I decided to let this earlier ambition serve my next ambition. You can do the same.

As a lawyer, I made enough money to support my family and give some away. With this, we took a deep dive into the lives of people laboring under unthinkable circumstances. While my early ambition to be a lawyer was good and right and helpful, it wasn't long before my new ambition of helping kids outdistanced my ability to earn money practicing law. This will happen to you, too, as you evolve.

It wasn't that my decision to become a lawyer was a bad one. After a while, the differences I made as a lawyer just didn't seem as significant or lasting to me as the differences I could make helping kids. So one day I quit my job as a lawyer—and it was my own law firm. That's right. I walked into my own law firm, got everyone together in a conference room, and said I was done. I gave the key to the front door to a guy who had worked there for a long time. I told him he didn't owe me anything for the company. I walked out, and I've never gone back. This probably sounds like a really stupid economic decision to some, and perhaps it was, but it was a terrific new creation decision.

If you've got a big decision you need to make to launch your ambition, go "new creation." We can't be the new version of us if we're stuck being an old version, and we're going to need to change some things that have worked in our past in order to make way for our future. Cut those past capabilities and ambitions loose or put them in service to the new ambitions you're chasing.

One last thing. Because we're meant to change, don't resist it when a little change comes your way. Embrace it. Celebrate it. Keep up with it. Stop freaking out about it. This is your chance to show the world you really believe in what you're doing.

If we're going to get after our ambitions, we need to be self-aware enough to know where lasting joy and sustained hope come from. We also need to know what things we're good at and what we're bad at. Our experiences will help point these things out. Beware of false positives. The affirmation we get from those things we're good at can mask the changes we still need to make to respond to the desires emerging within us. If we're limited to merely operating within our old capabilities, we'll never get to the new creation our ambitions are guiding us toward.

Chapter 9

SLEEPWALKING

Being fully awake looks a lot like
staying completely engaged.

I have often wrestled with insomnia. In truth, I've napped more than slept for most of my life. One upshot of being a light sleeper is I always knew when the kids got home at night. I wasn't upset if they missed curfew or anything, but I was just glad they were back with us.

When our son, Rich, was still living under our roof in high school, he had a semi-regular habit. He was a sleepwalker. One night I heard creaks in the stairs leading down from his bedroom. I grabbed my confetti cannon and got up to check out the noise, and I saw Rich coming down the stairs in his boxers, sound asleep. He opened the front door, went outside, and walked out to the end of the driveway. I didn't want him landing in jail all alone, so I followed him outside in my boxers too. There we were, father and son, standing outside in our underwear. I'm certain it was at least a misdemeanor.

I remembered something about sleepwalking from a college psychology class, and I took shaking him awake off the table because I learned it could be weirdly traumatic. Truth be told, I love Rich, but I didn't want him living with us when he was fifty years old, so I stood there patiently with him until he turned around and headed back inside. I escorted him to the bottom of the stairs, watched him go back up to his room, and shut the door behind him.

Each morning after one of Rich's nighttime strolls, I'd ask with a grin, "How'd you sleep, buddy?"

"Like a rock," he'd say, getting a good stretch in and reaching for the Cheerios. *Not,* I'd think.

Then I'd ask him if he felt a little draft while he slept, and he would look at me oddly because that's what high school kids do with their dads.

I chuckle at those memories. However, it's one thing to sleep-walk at one in the morning. It's another thing entirely to sleepwalk in the middle of your day. People do it all the time; maybe you do too. Who knows—maybe you're sleepwalking right now as you read this book.

If we're honest, *sleepwalking* describes many of our lives. You look like you're awake while you're not; you walk around talking to people while you're out cold. We get up, we walk, we talk, we do our jobs, and we go back to bed never having been fully awake. You'll know this is happening to you if you look back on your day and can't remember the conversations you've had, the things you experienced, and the beauty you saw. Perhaps you can't even remember the last chapter of this book you're reading.

When I was growing up, each of us grandkids had a room in my grandparents' house. On the wall of my room was a print of a priceless painting from the 1800s called "The Sleeping Cardinal." My grandmother picked up a copy at a yard sale for three dollars, including the frame. The image depicts an artist painting a portrait of the cardinal of a church.

What catches my eye immediately about this artwork is the painter's puzzled look—in it, he's scratching his head with palette in hand. The cardinal is slumped down in the chair, fast asleep, his chin resting on his red robe. I think God sometimes sees us and wonders the same thing the artist was wondering. *I'm creating a masterpiece here. When is this person going to wake up?*

What would our lives look like if we were fully awake to them? I wonder what would happen if we lived like insomniacs who couldn't shut our eyes to the wonders God was constantly showing us. At least the artist knew the cardinal was asleep. Sometimes we think we're giving the world the awake version of us when we're not.

The painful truth is that a form of sleepwalking may be getting in the way of your ambitions. Actually, it's more sinister than that. It's not stopping you on the way to the starting line; it's keeping you from even getting your jersey and running shoes on. The fix is as simple as it is hard. We need to wake up. This is going to take more than just smelling the coffee. It means getting out of bed, planting some coffee trees, having some patience, picking the beans, doing the roasting, and grinding them into something more useful.

Take the next step. Don't just look awake; come alive to who God has made you to be. Practice walking around fully awake to yourself. Take notes, sing songs, laugh a lot, smell the flowers, roll on the grass, write the letter, take the class, make the call. You're not doing this just for fun; it's one of your first steps as you wake up to some of your slumbering ambitions.

There are thirty-seven recorded miracles in the New Testament. One of my personal practices is to memorize each of them. Try it some-time. It will bring tremendous focus to your day and meaning to your interactions, and it will amplify your faith. Here's how to do it. Almost everyone knows the first miracle Jesus did, right? There was a wedding celebration and they ran out of wine. Jesus took some jars of water, turned them into wine, and the party kept going. What I've been looking at aren't just the miracles, but what was happening *around* the miracles. At the wedding, Mary leaned over to the host after he spoke to Jesus and whispered, "Do whatever he tells you." This is my hope for you as you pursue your ambitions. Whether faith is important to you or not, whether you talk to Jesus all the time or almost never, I hope you will take the ideas in these pages about pursuing your ambitions and then do whatever God tells you to do with them.

I'm a meat-and-potatoes guy when it comes to faith. I don't see ladybugs landing on my nose as a message from God. I'm confident if God had a message for me and I missed it, He knows where I live and would send an elephant to land on me next time. Still, I enter each day assuming there's a thirty-eighth miracle waiting for me if I'll fully engage life and the people around me with love, honesty, and an unreasonable, almost annoying heap of expectation. What would happen in your life if you started doing the same?

If you want to make progress toward your ambitions, live in con-stant anticipation of what might happen next. Look constantly for opportunities to give your ambitions some lift, and when an opening comes along, be ready to do something about it. People who actively anticipate opportunities don't just sit on the edge of the chair hoping. They stack books on the chair and stand on top of them looking for an opportunity. Try it. The view will be great.

∽

As you identify and pursue your ambitions, don't be alarmed or discouraged when things get uncomfortable. The truth is, you're probably going to need to make a couple of easy things uncomfortable. If you're going to live fully awake and full of anticipation, you need to spot those areas in your current life where you've slipped into numbing routines that are putting you to sleep.

Perhaps the routines that once brought some positive rhythms to your day have become a bland, enslaving drumbeat. Here are some telltale signs. Maybe you have become generally dissatisfied and listless. Perhaps you're short with the people you love or respond to small inconveniences with disproportionate annoyance. If this is you, you've got three choices: wake up, chill out, or get a puppy. You can have ours. If you want to press through the resistance you're facing, you need to identify your own "tells" like a good poker player.

To do this, you'll need to do a little excavation and take some action to figure out what is keeping you stuck. You may have to break with some routines, identify some of the stress in your life, and get the tools you need to clarify your ambitions. I'm not suggesting you blow up your whole life. But doing something startling to shake yourself awake should definitely be on the table.

Do you need to quit your job or change your major? Do you need to ask her out on a date or hit the pause button on your relationship? Do you need to have *the talk* with him? Do you need to downsize your house to free up money to fund your dream? Do you need to hire someone to help or invite someone to live in your guest house because they need a leg up in their life? It could be any of a million things you need to do.

I've learned that pursuing our ambitions isn't a walk in the park; it's an assault on a tall mountain. Sometimes you'll find yourself hanging by crimped fingertips on the cliff face. Don't back off. This is normal. Don't get me wrong, normal doesn't mean *pleasant*, it just means *common* for the people who will to take the risks necessary to get after their ambitions.

ဆ

When you get fired up about your ambitions, it's tempting to think you need to spring-load your mattress and start each day with crazy momentum. Who knows? Perhaps some days you'll wake up, step onto your back porch, and beat your chest and yell like a warrior. (If this is you, get some blue face paint and a kilt and go full *Braveheart* a couple of times. Your neighbors will think you're crazy. It'll be great.) One lesson I've learned, though, is that sometimes the best way to make progress is by sitting still. It feels counterintuitive, but it's true.

Any person I've ever known who's chased and accomplished an ambition knew that some days were about gathering strength instead of exerting it. Make no mistake—it's easy to confuse a lot of activity with a bunch of progress. Rest is wise; preparation is wisdom. Don't think that taking care of yourself—lying down for the nap, lounging in the hammock, or sitting on the park bench—means you're slacking. Stop reading the junk mail telling you this. You're not a startup and you don't sleep under your desk. You're on a mission, but you're not lazy when you rest. You're plotting your next moves and giving yourself the strength and perspective needed to finish the course. The path to your ambitions is not one long race; it's a series of wind sprints that eventually covers the distance of a marathon. There's a reason sprinters don't break world records in five-thousand-meter races. They stay focused and run their short race then rest before their next one.

People who refuse to rest eventually run out of steam. They get sick or procrastinate or rationalize the defeat. The reason for their failure is simple: they're winded. Their constant activity actually has them sleepwalking again. They know they don't have the energy to see it through, and they start deferring their ambitions. Part of the process of realizing your ambitions is recognizing when you need a break. If a break is what you need, take one. It's not just okay; it's smart. Get as much rest as you need. You'll know when it's time to be fully awake and get back to work.

Chapter 10

ONE HUNDRED CALLS A DAY

Availability is your secret weapon.

I put my cell phone number in the back of all the books I write. It's in the back of this one too. Call me to tell me how things are going in your journey. The first time I did this, my publisher thought I was crazy—and, on reflection, they were right. It's been almost a decade since my first book, and I still get one hundred calls a day on average. I can't get a thing done. It's terrific. Here's why I did it: our availability to one another is a pretty good measure of how available we will be to opportunities that come our way. Far from being a nuisance, each of these phone calls is a reminder and has been the best part of writing books.

I get calls at all hours of the day and night from new and old friends around the world. Sometimes it will be a witch doctor at one of our schools in Uganda, where we teach them to read and write, and other times it's a new friend in need a little closer to home. I once got a call from a woman who said she'd received my book on her birthday.

"Honey, this book is going to change the rest of my life!" she almost shouted into the telephone.

"Happy birthday!" I said. "How old are you?"

"One hundred and four!" she yelped.

You go girl!

Sometimes taking the calls can be costly. One time, a college kid in Michigan backed her car into someone else's in a parking lot. This student was broke and afraid to leave her phone number under the windshield wiper of the damaged car because she couldn't afford to fix it. She had my book in her car so she left my number instead. I got a call in San Diego a day later from an agitated person in Michigan and was so impressed by the boldness of the student's move that I bought the guy a new fender. It was an expensive day, but I knew I'd have a story to tell, so it was worth it.

Availability is the most reliable predictor of engagement, and engagement will be the most reliable predictor of success. None of us can decide how tall or short we'll be, what color hair we'll have, or the year we will be born, but we can decide how available we'll be. Have you noticed that people who seem to accomplish the most always seem to have time for almost anything? It's like they manufacture the stuff in a room behind their houses. Availability can be a huge multiplier in your life. You'll meet more people, get more invitations, and more opportunities will come your way. I decided to be überavailable even before there was a company called Uber. Perhaps you should, too, if you want to pursue your ambitions. Here's why. People don't follow vision; they follow availability. There's no economic barrier to get there. Usually, all it will cost you is your pride.

A man with only a few days to live called me from his hospital room. It was a sacred conversation I still remember to this day. I would have missed it if I had not been available. Another time, a couple of girls in Texas were driving on the highway and their car broke down. They didn't have roadside assistance, but they had my book and knew I was in their area at a speaking event, so they called. We found them on the highway and fixed the car. I considered it my personal best. Fortunately, it was a new battery cable they needed, not a rebuilt transmission.

Our ambitions should point toward the legacy we want to leave behind. Aiming for a legacy of generosity, where you give away both your time and talent, isn't a bad place to start. Maybe you need to start taking more calls. Doing this will probably lead toward one of the values you want to be known for now and remembered for later. I decided I wanted to be known as the guy who was always available. For me, meeting new people stokes new perspectives and curiosity. Understanding how others have engaged in their lives will awaken something inside of you too. Simply put, no one going after a big ambition is going to get there on their own.

Availability means more than just being available to everyone else; you also need to stay available to yourself. Sometimes we go through a day doing all the things we've committed to or that were expected of us without really "checking in" with ourselves. *How am I feeling? Does God feel near? Am I living out my top priorities and most beautiful ambitions through my choices and actions?* Certainly no one does this perfectly. I don't, and you won't either. Still, the people who tune into their ambitions check in with themselves often. How about you? Do you stay available and self-aware, or do you give yourself away willy-nilly to everything and everyone else? It isn't selfish to ask these questions, by the way. It's evidence of emotional maturity and self-assuredness.

One of the first things they teach you when you are learning to fly a plane is situational awareness. It means being aware of what's going on both inside and outside the cockpit. It is about knowing what is happening now and anticipating what will happen next, while remaining undistracted by either. We could all use a little of this.

When you get laser-focused on your ambitions and your whole life is angling toward them, you'll see more clearly which of your current commitments and choices are launching you forward and which are standing in the way of your progress. Stop for a moment and recognize this, then develop some situational awareness as you prepare to do something about it. I'll cover this more in later chapters. For now, though, start to become aware of yourself. Ask yourself these questions: Am I feeling safe, supported, known? Am I expressing myself authentically, or have my interactions felt artificial and contrived? Am I saying what I really think, or am I channeling someone else's explanation about life that I don't fully believe?

Even if this feels a little foreign, carve that new groove in your brain and check in with yourself more often. People who achieve their ambitions are constantly doing this. It becomes so natural that after a while they're unaware they're doing it anymore. It just becomes part of how they roll.

One of my favorite stories about availability is the two boys who gave their lunches to Jesus to feed the people who had followed Him out into a field. We don't know if they were brothers or buddies, but I've always assumed they were friends. It became a defining moment for them, yet it probably wasn't their intention that morning to cater a meal for five thousand. Instead, I bet it was simply their moms' intentions to pack them a lunch that day—because that's what moms often do. We don't know the names of the boys or of the moms, but they weren't looking for recognition. The people who are prepared and available like those two boys—and the ones who are taking care of business, like their moms—are the ones who have stories repeated about them for generations. Their moms were probably aware of what was going on around them and the needs these two boys had for a lunch. These two boys were prepared and available. They were situationally aware. They knew what they had, and they were willing to give it to Jesus when He asked. You'll need to be equally ready. If you'll do this (and pack a lunch), you might make history too.

In the Benedictine tradition, some monks have the job of being a "porter." I had always thought of a porter as a Sherpa who could carry my latte machine up Everest. However, for the Benedictines, a porter's job is to get up early each day, walk down to the city gate, and greet people. Porters ask travelers this question: "What can I do to help you on your way?" Taking an interest in people means asking the same. If you want to make progress on your ambitions, ask other people about theirs. It was this kind of reverse economy Jesus spoke about often. It worked then, and it works now.

Jesus didn't hide from people. He didn't have any middlemen, and perhaps you shouldn't either. Sure, He spent time alone, but it wasn't long before everyone showed up. He didn't have someone vetting everyone who came His way either. I have a couple of friends who put loads of barriers between themselves and everyone else under the banner of efficiency. That's fine, I suppose, if that is the messaging you want to release into the world. But what is efficient isn't always effective. The people you spend time with will play the largest part in the ambitions you achieve, not the minutes you saved each day by avoiding them. Be available. Talk to everyone. Become their student, not their teacher. Love's goal isn't ever efficiency; it's presence.

Being more available isn't about networking. Networking is for rookies. When you blow the foam off the top, networking is nothing more than pretending to be friends *with* someone while having a secret agenda *for* someone. You'll know you're fully available when there's nothing on the other side of the equals sign of availability—just you and your big, beautiful ambitions as well as a load of interest in what other people's ambitions are too.

You're going to find the path toward your ambitions as you make yourself available to the people you meet along the way. Being available isn't about giving yourself away recklessly or wearing yourself down to the point where you have no energy to do your own work. It's about keeping yourself open to the world around you so you don't fall back asleep.

One last thing. Remember what you've made yourself available to. Write down what you learn. I send myself between 100 and 150 emails a day. When I get home at night, I check my emails and see all the ones from me, and I'm tempted to block myself. Here's why I don't. I get a second shot at learning what I've written down. I answer the phone with my left hand because I have a pen in my right hand to take notes. The trick for leading a noteworthy life is having noteworthy conversations and writing down what you learn. Do lots of that and opportunities will find you. Availability attracts ideas. Write down the good ones, and you will gain clarity on your ambitions.

Chapter 11

SEA OTTERS

Hold on tight to a couple of people.

There is a city called Buford in Wyoming. It's the smallest city in the country. Actually, only one person lives there, and he's thinking about moving—it's just getting too crowded. God, though, always does His best work in community. Adam was the first man alive, and God said it wasn't good that he was alone. He still feels the same. God gives us people so we can practice and understand our humanity and our faith. Cultivating a community isn't just a way to avoid loneliness; it's the method we use to interpret our own lives. If you have a solid community, grow it and let other people join in. Don't be an exclusive clique for a few; be a gathering place for many. They need community as much as you do. If you're still looking for a posse, look harder. It's worth all the effort you'll give it. Besides, if you don't want to be around people, you're going to hate heaven. We're all practicing for eternity together.

The power of community is immense. I was speaking to a group of people who were very conservative in their views. Near the end, the people who attended my talk were invited to text in questions that would be put on a screen behind me so we could discuss the top couple of questions. The people in the audience could vote up or vote down the questions on the screen to decide which ones had the greatest collective interest. One of the first questions on the screen was from someone who texted this: "I'm all alone, I'm gay, and I just don't know what to do." Twenty other questions came in over the next ten minutes. Each one trended up, while this first question sank lower on the screen until it was dead last.

I'm a lawyer and win arguments for a living. That said, I don't court controversy, particularly in matters of faith and practice. That doesn't make me soft on Scripture; it makes me big on Jesus. While we shouldn't be known for our combative opinions, the reality is sometimes there are challenging issues that we need to talk about so they don't distract and divide us. We can ignore these difficult conversations completely, but only for a while and at great risk. The better alternative is to engage them with kindness and love whenever possible.

I see myself as a follower *of* Jesus, not a lawyer *for* Him. I've got a lot of confidence in the power of truth. Truth has power and doesn't need as much defense as we sometimes act like it needs. Peter told his friends to be ready to make a defense for the hope within them; he also said to do it "with gentleness and respect." Sometimes it seems people in faith communities are drawn more to "making a defense" than the "gentleness and respect" part. We can pick our fights by being picky about the questions we ask. Did you know that Jesus asked more than three hundred questions and only answered two? Be picky about the questions you answer as well.

That night onstage, I glanced back at the list of questions on the screen and pulled a page from Jesus' playbook. I inverted the list and asked everyone to lean in on the least popular question that night, not the most popular. What I experienced wasn't hostility and animus. I didn't see people who wanted to be "right." The room was filled with people who wanted to be human. Equal parts of wisdom, love, and acceptance flooded into the room. Sure, there were people who perhaps disagreed with parts of this person's lifestyle, or bristled at the issue, but they also understood the power of love. I wasn't their leader that night; I was their student. It turned out to be a beautiful evening where I witnessed a community come together and lead with love.

After the evening had wrapped up and everyone had left, a young man came up to me. He said it was his question that had been voted down to the bottom and he told me that as he watched the ranking drop, he felt like he wasn't just losing a popularity contest—he was losing any chance at community and belonging. He questioned the value of being alive as he watched his question get voted down. Then a community filled with love and compassion and Jesus arrived. They literally saved his life. Loving people the way Jesus did is always great theology.

Know your beliefs. Understand them. Devote yourself to them. Then take all of that and make it your ambition to be part of a loving community, and you will live well. Jesus loves all of us equally. There will be people you disagree with, and more than a couple of people are going to disagree with you. If you want to access your ambitions, place a high value on community and kindness and you will find them.

Community doesn't always have to feel this heavy. It can be beautiful. I try to find reminders about the power we can experience together everywhere. When we're in Canada, we see thousands of sea otters drifting along on the top of the water in the inlet. They're everywhere—kind of like Priuses. Did you know sea otters hold hands while they're floating? It looks a lot like they're going out on dates with each other. After seeing so many sea otter couples drifting two by two through the water, I figured there had to be some reason for the hand holding. I dug a little deeper and it turns out the answer is simple: *they don't want anyone to drift away.*

As you pursue your ambitions, you're going to need some hands to hold and some friends to love so you don't drift off into the open waters. In other words, you're going to need a community if you want to achieve something outrageous with your life. If we want to build an authentic community, we've got to do a better job getting to know each other.

Did you know a handful of sand has about four hundred thousand grains in it? I haven't counted, but Wikipedia wouldn't lie to me. If you live for ninety-two years and have twelve conversations a day, that's about four hundred thousand conversations in a lifetime. How many of these do you want to spend talking about the weather? We'll meet a lot of people in a lifetime, but how many will we truly get to know? If you want to narrow the gap between you and your ambitions, try going a little deeper with the people you encounter and definitely with the people God has already placed closest to you.

Try to have twelve real conversations a day. Not *How are you doing?* or *Where do you work?* or *What team are you cheering for?* Start with the fourth, fifth, and sixth questions. Here are some examples. *Who are you? What are the things you want in life? How is it really going?* Go to questions like *What was the high and low for you this week or this month? When was the last time you felt lonely? When was the last time you laughed so hard you peed yourself?* Seriously, try it with your Uber driver or with the person next to you on an airplane. Elevators, too, I suppose. If you ask a stranger a considerate, authentic, and engaging question and are willing to match or exceed the vulnerability you're pursuing, you will be absolutely amazed at the depth and richness you'll discover just below the surface of their life. Be kind and respectful as you do this. Don't try to go too deep too quick or you'll just get the bends like an overeager scuba diver. Don't settle for just treading water on the surface either.

We all spend a lot of time talking about surface things with each other. I get why. A cocktail of fear and politeness and insecurity keeps us there. If we're going to carve a new groove in our brains and go Grand Canyon on them, we're going to need to start doing a few things differently. We need to stop hiding behind our appearances and titles and accomplishments and successes. Keep this in mind: if you take away what you're known for, whatever is left is who you are. Let's be the kind of people who are more interested in who someone *is* instead of what they *do*.

I went to a place called Onsite outside of Nashville for some counseling, and one of the only rules they had was that no one could ask anyone else what they do for a living. Find out about someone's character, not just their career. Don't just agree with Onsite that this is a good idea. Do it with someone today. It'll blow both of you away. The adventure on your way toward your ambitions is going to require a new level of authenticity with yourself and interest in the people around you. Keep it real with each other and with God. Jesus didn't have a problem with people who were confused or discouraged; He just wanted people to be authentic. He'll take real over confident any day.

∽

On my most recent trip to Africa, I was attacked by the most vicious animal on the continent. It wasn't a rhino or an elephant or a cobra (all of which are still on my bucket list)—it was a mosquito. No kidding. I've been traveling to Africa for the last twenty years. I usually go a few times a year, and while they recommend taking malaria medicine, I never take it. I mean, who needs it, right? I didn't skip the pills because they were expensive or inconvenient. The pills are cheap, and if you take just one a day, you won't have any problems. Still, I waved it all off as unnecessary. Almost predictably, I got malaria. Almost a million people die each year of malaria, so it's not something you want to get. If you get the aggressive form of malaria, starting with your liver and kidneys, your body starts going offline one organ at a time until you get the right meds or you're dead.

The crazy thing is that I didn't know I had malaria, so I kept up my travel and speaking schedule. Two countries and eight cities later, it had almost killed me. I ended up in the hospital, and from my bed, I heard a doctor say to Sweet Maria, within earshot of me, that I had a one in three chance of surviving. I think I heard one of the nurses call dibs on my shoes.

I was in the ICU for a week. The great part about getting malaria is that I lost thirty pounds. Forget all those weight-loss books. My next book isn't even going to have words in it—just one hungry mosquito with an attitude and a virus. We got the bill for my time in the hospital, and it was more than I paid for our first house. Here's the thing. I could have avoided all this with a nickel pill and half a glass of water. You can avoid some of the stuff that's distracting you from your ambitions just as simply.

Small things become big things. Jesus told His friends nothing less. He talked about mustard seeds and said they were the smallest kind of seed. The fact is, they're not. Because I'm a lawyer, I checked. The smallest seed in the world is a Peruvian orchid. It weighs less than one twenty-four millionths of an ounce. The story isn't about the seed though; it's about the tree it grows into and the rest it gives to those who need it most. I've done a couple of big things but a lot more small ones. You have too. God can use both, I suppose, but I think He delights in the small stuff a lot more.

Other than my kidneys being permanently shot, I'm just fine after getting malaria. I've crossed kidneys off of my donor card. They're just no good anymore. I'm trying to grow a strong heart to make up for it.

If you hold out your left hand in front of you, I bet it will be as steady as mine is. I could do Lasik surgery on anyone with eyeballs right handed. Since the tussle with malaria, my left hand has a very noticeable tremor. When it really gets shaking, I could whip eggs with it.

I was in Washington, DC, for some meetings with friends who were doing important things. As the meeting wrapped up, someone said, "Let's all hold hands and pray." I was a little surprised in the context, but a circle was already forming. Instead of reaching out, I put both hands in my pockets to cover up my shaky left one. I didn't want the people there to think I was weak. I also didn't want them to think I was intimidated being with them. How stupid is that? Jesus performed His seventh miracle when He met a guy who had a problem with his hand. I doubt it was from malaria, but maybe he had his hands in his pockets too. Shame, embarrassment, and feeling inferior will do this to us. Jesus said to the man, "Stretch out your hand."

Jesus could have fixed the man's hand while it was in his pocket, but He didn't. I think Jesus wanted this guy to take the kind of action I hope you'll be willing to take. I realized I've spent my whole life reaching out my strong hand to people. It seems counterintuitive, but if you're doing the same, it might be getting in the way of your ambitions. Here's a suggestion that will work every time. Reach out a weaker, more authentic hand to people you meet. Sure, it's easy to reach out your strong hand, the one that is confident and steady. It takes a little more guts to reach out your weak hand. It's the kind of move that will shape your character while making you more available to the people and things that matter most in your life.

Chapter 12

FINALE

Taking a genuine interest in others'
ambitions can unleash yours.

P aul was talking behind the back of one of his friends named
Timothy. What he said about him gives all of us something to
shoot for in our lives. Paul said Timothy was a guy who took a genuine
interest in the people around him. I love that. More than a reminder
to just say something nice about someone like Paul did, it's the path
we all must take to achieve our ambitions. We need to take a genuine
interest in the people around us. *But wait. I thought this was about
helping me achieve my ambitions, not having me help others advance theirs.*

One day I was sitting with a friend of mine, and he leaned over
and passed me his cell phone to show me a text message he'd just
received.

"Do you know who Bob Goff is?"

I chuckled and handed the phone back to him. He smiled and texted back, "Bob Goff is sitting right next to me."

A few moments later, he handed me the phone again. "Will you ask Bob if he'll write the foreword to my book?"

The guy sending the text was Greg Murtha. He was the driving force behind Bob Buford's Halftime movement, which has helped a lot of people think about their lives in terms of significance instead of success. Greg was a behind-the-scenes guy for a lot of other meaningful ventures, and while he always took a big step away from the spotlight, he remained an exceptionally bright light in the world.

What I didn't know as the text messages came in was that Greg was on his death bed. He had cancer and had been through almost one hundred rounds of chemotherapy. He knew he would be dancing with Jesus within the next couple of days.

I don't have the time I wish I had to write forewords for people's books. I labor over every word, and it takes me days. But I knew if I said no to Greg a trap door would probably open and I'd go straight to hell without even dying first. So I immediately texted him back on my friend's phone and said, "Greg, this is Bob and I'd be honored to write your foreword."

A few days later Greg passed and began his eternity-long dance with Jesus. But I had a problem. I'd only met Greg one time. To write the foreword well, I would need to get to know Greg a little better through the people who knew him best. For the next several weeks, I called his friends and asked them to tell me about Greg. Do you know what they all said? Literally every single person said Greg was a guy who took a genuine interest in the people around him.

Do you want to make some of your big ambitions happen? Be like Greg. Be like Timothy. Take a genuine interest in the people around you. Make it what you're known for. Make it your defining characteristic. Make it your anthem. You might think that achieving your ambitions means keeping your head down, battening down the hatches, and shutting others out so you can get more important work done. Don't fall for it. Ambitions don't flow from the quantity of our ideas or our uninterrupted drive; they gush out from our kindness and willingness to take a genuine interest in others.

Jesus gave us some instructions on how His backwards economy would operate. Do you want to be rich? *Give away what you have.* Do you want status? *Lose all of yours.* Do you want to lead? *Learn how to follow.* Do you want to achieve your big ambitions? *Help others to achieve theirs.*

Ruth did it with Naomi, Aaron did it with Moses, Jesus did it with Lazarus and Zacchaeus and the woman at the well and the guy on the cross next to Him and everyone else He met. It'll be a good place for you to start too.

∽

When I was young, someone took an interest in me. I was about eight years old, had flaming red hair, and was absolutely covered in freckles. A bully who lived nearby constantly made fun of them. This bully gave me the nickname "Spot." It's my earliest memory of feeling shame. After getting heckled and put down day after day by this person, I didn't like my freckles or the guy they were covering. I remember sitting in my bedroom with an eraser trying to make the spots disappear. I did this for hours until I bled. I wasn't cutting; I was erasing, but it had the same effect.

All this changed when a person came along who took a genuine interest in me and my freckles. One day this person came into my room and told me to stretch out my arms. With Sharpie in hand, they started to draw little lines between the dots on my arms. I wasn't quite sure what to do, so I just let them keep drawing. Once enough lines were connected between my freckles, I saw an image starting to take shape. As this person capped the Sharpie, I looked down at my arms and saw a couple of towering giraffes. I was the first kid in class to have some ink on his arms. For the first time, instead of seeing spots, I saw endless possibilities. I stopped seeing defects; I saw puzzles to figure out, zoo animals to find, opportunities to discover. I eventually realized this kind person who took an interest in me wasn't teaching me to see giraffes at all, but to accept and celebrate myself for who I am, spots and all.

Maybe you've had some people put you down too. You have your own freckles, whatever they may be and wherever they came from in your past. I've changed my mind about my freckles. Now I think they were just God getting a little excited with the paint brush when He made me. It's the same for you. He painted a bit of Himself on your canvas—a wild, extravagantly unique, one-of-a-kind expression. Don't let anyone convince you your freckles are spots to be ashamed of; they're reminders that you're loved.

➴

A little later in life, a friend of mine named Don took a genuine interest in me. I met Don years ago when he was kayaking by my family's Lodge in Canada. As he paddled closer and we shot saltwater taffy at him with slingshots, we figured out he and his friends were doing a long-distance trip. They looked hungry, so we invited them up to our house. At the time we met and I was launching taffy at him, he was just a moving target. Later I learned that Don was a *New York Times* bestselling author who had impacted a lot of people with his books. Over the years, he became a dear friend.

As I got to know Don, I started to see how big his heart was and how creatively he engaged with the world. One of my secret ambitions was to be an author, but I hesitated to speak this out loud to an *actual* bestselling author. How many times do we avoid asking the question to the very person God just put in our path with the answer?

Our friendship grew, and one day I got up the courage to tell him I wanted to write a book. I dialed it back a little, looking at my feet with my hands in my pockets, and said sheepishly, "I'd love to write down some stories to share with my kids and Sweet Maria someday." He stopped what he was doing, looked at me square in the eye, and said, "That's a really beautiful ambition, Bob, but what if we create something that lands on the *New York Times* bestseller list and encourages even more people?" *That's impossible,* I thought to myself. *I can barely spell* cat.

Don was subtly, kindly daring me to grasp my ambition. But he didn't stop there. He started to share what he'd learned about writing and how to go about the process, which was a complete mystery to me. This is what friends do. They draw your ambitions out of you and make you feel safe enough to assemble the wheels on them and roll them out.

Some time passed, and I was preparing to start my book-writing process. Around the same time I took a trip to Portland, where Don was speaking at a conference. I wanted to see him in his element.

After Don finished his time onstage, we went to a room where a couple of friends were waiting. When we got there, Don put a hand on each of my shoulders, looked me in the eyes, and in an unusually serious voice said, "Bob, writing this book is going to be the loneliest, hardest thing you'll ever do."

Loneliest? Hardest? Yikes. I thought it was supposed to be fun.

Then Don pulled out a big box full of neatly wrapped gifts. Each one had a tag with a message on it. I felt like a kid at Christmas. The tags corresponded to different steps and phases in the writing process. I didn't even know what they meant. Don said, "When you get to each of these stages, you can open the box and celebrate the progress you've made." There was a box to open when I finished a chapter, when I turned in the book, and when I read the book out loud to my family. It was incredibly motivating and inspiring. Don's kindness was pouring jet fuel onto my ambition.

Over the next several months, Don and I Skyped once a week, and I told him how the writing was going. I let him know the words were hard to find, the ones I had written were uninspiring, and most of them were misspelled. No matter what I said, he told me I was doing great. I shared with him that rereading my words was torture. Don responded by telling me that's exactly how I was supposed to feel and it was a really great sign that I felt like hurling. I'm certain if I had told him I was bleeding from my nose, ears, and forehead, he would have said this is exactly what all great writers experience. Don kept reminding me that writing a book is not for the faint of heart; it's for the strong in character. He told me the reasons behind my ambitions were worth the effort and not to get distracted by the typos but to delight in my attempts. He said success would be found by people who remained certain about why they are doing what they're doing. It wasn't lost on me that he always pointed me toward the purpose *behind* my ambition, not the ambition itself.

Whenever I finished a chapter, I would email it to Don. He only ever gave me two responses. If he liked the chapter, he would write back one word: "finale." I'm not sure why he used that word, but it meant the chapter was a keeper. If Don didn't think a chapter was strong enough, he'd write back and say, "Maria's going to love this chapter." This actually meant the pages were neither fit to print nor burn. I wrote a lot of words that Maria was apparently going to love. Every once in a while, though, I'd get a "finale" from Don. Along the way I'd open the presents he thoughtfully chose for me. When I got about thirty "finales," I turned in the book and opened the second-to-last present.

The last present from Don was waiting for when the first printed book arrived in the mail from the publisher. When that day came, I patched in Don so we could cross the finish line together. I flipped the pages to smell the fresh ink and opened the last package. It was a medal. Sweet Maria pinned it in on my chest as Don spoke the same words of love and encouragement that got me started a year before. Without Don I probably never would have written a book. Without him, you certainly wouldn't be holding this book right now.

That first book was called *Love Does*. It was on *New York Times* bestsellers list for many months. The next book, *Everybody Always*, was the result of another friend named Bryan, who believed in me and also helped me find better words. That book also found its way onto the *New York Times* bestsellers list. We've sold over a million copies of *Love Does* and have given away every penny to start schools for kids in conflict areas. Do you know why? I had an ambition. Someone named Don and another friend named Bryan pulled behind it. When I wanted to bail, they reminded me of the purpose behind my efforts. And they did it because they were listening to me and took a genuine interest in what I was trying to do.

Isn't it a beautiful thing when we give away our love and expertise to help someone with their ambitions? No one—absolutely *no one*—goes from daydreaming about their ambition to living out the dream without others getting into the mix. Surround yourself with a Don or three. Become a Bryan for a couple of people you meet. This is where we find the keys to unlock our greatest achievements.

Because of Don and Bryan's examples, I started to look for ways to make things happen for other people with their own ambitions. I began carrying medals around with me. I've given away thousands of them. I've been listening closely to people, just like Don and Bryan listened to me. I've tried to create for other people the kind of safe spots that others made for me where I could say out loud what I had only been dreaming about. I've taken a genuine interest in others the way many people have taken a genuine interest in me. And I've wrapped more than a few presents for others simply because someone did it for me when I need a little encouragement.

One last quick story. I was flying to Springfield, Illinois, and a guy across the aisle was reading a book I'd written. I had never seen anybody reading it in the wild before, so I took a picture and put it up on Instagram with the simple caption, "There's a guy reading my book!" Lots of people immediately posted comments. Most of them said, "You've got to meet him." But I didn't want to be "that guy." You know, the weirdo who wants to tell you all about himself. I was having an animated debate in my mind. *Should I talk to him? Should I pass by? What if he thinks I'm a weirdo? Wait, I am a weirdo.* I decided not to say anything on the airplane.

We landed, and I followed him out of the plane and into the airport terminal. After walking a while, he put his carry-ons down and started rifling through one of them. I walked up to him, debated with myself again briefly, then threw my arms in the air and half-shouted, "I wrote the book you were reading!" He looked at me and started shaking. He looked like he was going to have a stroke. This was not going well. I asked, a little concerned, "Buddy, are you okay?" He just stared at me blankly and eventually said, "No! My wife gave me this stupid book to read, and it turns out it's about Jesus, which I don't get. But now you're telling me you wrote it and you were sitting behind me on the airplane. It's like God is stalking me!" I told him my cell number was on the back of the book and to call me any time. We said a quick prayer together and each headed out our own way.

I stayed in touch with my new friend from the airport. A while later, I went back to Springfield where he got baptized. I took a genuine interest in him because he was reading a book that was written because someone took a genuine interest in me.

Like this encounter at the airport, I've experienced thousands of chance intersections that helped both myself and others move from the bleachers to the field. You have too. I've been inspired and cried and prayed with strangers. I've witnessed countless dreams come true and seen people become better friends with Jesus. All this happened for one simple reason: someone took a genuine interest in me. It's a power we equally possess if we'll decide to access it.

Chapter 13

COMPARISON IS A PUNK

We can tie our hearts together without
tying our shoelaces together.

If we're going to do community well and take a genuine interest in others, there's a land mine I have to warn you about: comparison. These days it feels like all we see are people who are doing life better than us. You'll never find your purpose by comparing your life to someone else's. Don't you dare hold up your ambitions to someone else's and try to rank them like some kind of inspiration cage fight. All this said, you know what's crazy? I preach this stuff every day to others and yet I still find myself struggling with comparison. If I did one push-up for every time I compared my ambition to someone else's ambition, I'd be totally ripped.

When it comes to comparison, don't do it and don't fall for it.

Comparison is a punk. Look into the mirror a couple of times a day at that beautiful, God-given mug of yours and tell yourself over and over until you believe it that God never wondered if you had everything you needed to be fully you. We just need to get you on board with the idea that you are a wonderfully creative, totally fallible, gifted, easily distractible, once-ever-in-history you.

There is an Olympic athlete named Matt Emmons who is one of the best rifle marksmen in the world. He could take a hair off a flea at a hundred yards if fleas had hairs. In 2004, he represented the United States at the Olympics and had the gold medal sewn up. No one was even close to his points tally. He had one last shot, and then he could stroll over to the podium to receive his next medal. He could have hit anywhere on the target. The white part, the black part, anywhere.

He steadied himself, took a half a breath, and slowly let it out as he pulled the trigger. Once again, it was another dead-on bull's-eye. But there were no cheers, no clapping. It was total silence. Here's why. Matt was aiming at someone else's target. This is called "cross fire," and it doesn't happen often in the Olympics, but it happens every day in our lives. Like many of us, Matt hit the wrong target perfectly, but choosing someone else's bull's-eye cost him the win.

Paul wrote to his friends and told them something worth repeating here. He told them to live a life worthy of the calling *they* had received (Ephesians 4:1). In other words, aim for your own target, not everyone else's. If you want to do something that honors God, stop trying to be someone else and go be you. Figure out your own ambitions. Understand them. Own them. Take aim at them. Pull the trigger. Confusing someone else's dreams for your own, or thinking your dreams should be more like theirs, will cost you the prize. Every. Single. Time. God made you uniquely gifted. Go run your own race. We can tie our hearts together without tying our shoelaces together.

We all have wonderfully different ambitions. Aside from evil, morally wrong, harmful, or unjust ambitions, our part isn't to examine or score or handicap the ambitions of others. Tend to your own fire. Don't get on the same page with everyone else; get on your page. If you want to restore a plane, climb a mountain, raise llamas, or create a new element on the periodic table, go for it. Don't worry about building consensus around your idea and stop asking for permission; get busy with what's happening in your life and stop trying to figure out everyone else's.

If you find someone who wants the same things, you don't need to sync up with them, receive validation from them, or pursue agreement with them. Just delight in knowing you've found a kindred spirit. Sure, be likeminded. Be "one" the way Jesus said He wanted us to be, but don't make the mistake of thinking that "oneness" means "sameness." It doesn't.

Whatever dreams are bubbling up in your heart, there are probably a few people who have done something similar. Don't wave off because someone wrote a book on the same topic you wanted to write about. Most country and western songs can be played with the same three cords and have lyrics about a "big ole truck." That didn't keep Garth Brooks from writing his next one. Quit letting it stop you.

It's easy to fall into the trap of thinking you have to do things the way everyone else did. It's also tempting to think someone else had an easier path with smaller obstacles than the ones you're facing. Who knows, maybe they did. Chasing after your dreams requires clear-headedness and wide eyes that are trained to follow the specific path in front of *you*, not the path in front of them.

I met a woman named Grace who told me about her ambition. She is a woman of color who grew up facing down prejudice and other obstacles in her life. Yet she was so full of immense kindness and Jesus that there was no room left for guile or bitterness. Her ambition was to become a speaker so she could share what she had learned about love and acceptance and setbacks and Jesus. There are plenty of speakers who have faced similar setbacks. But what Grace needed was to run her own race and have some people take a genuine interest in her.

She had never really had a shot at speaking in front of a large crowd. Without a big stage with loads of cameras, she didn't have a video showing her speaking to demonstrate that she had what it took to get on other stages. It was a catch-22 that probably sounds familiar to anyone with a similar ambition. She didn't need more information about her ambition; she just needed an opportunity.

When Grace and I met, I was scheduled to speak to three thousand people a few days later. I knew there would be plenty of high-end video cameras pointed at the stage, so I invited Grace to join me. I didn't clear the idea with anyone first. We just walked out onto the stage holding hands. I walked with her to the microphone, whispered "go," and stepped out of the camera frame. I'll probably never get invited to speak there again, but you know what? Grace crushed it. It was the most inspired talk I've heard in ages. I wasn't surprised when everybody loved her. Grace speaks all over the place now.

She could have had a thousand and one complaints about the setbacks and barriers both behind and in front of her. She could have played the comparison game and thought everyone else had it easier or was a better speaker than she was. Instead, she walked her own path and it led her right to that microphone. She did her best and it was way more than enough. Listen closely. Your best is enough too.

There was another guy named Aaron who worked at my law firm for years as a paralegal. I asked him about his ambitions, and he told me he *really* wanted to be a lawyer. But he had a problem. He didn't have three years for law school; he had three kids and a wife. He also didn't have two hundred grand to spend on tuition at a fancy law school. So we went to the Washington State Bar Association. My law partner at the time, Danny, and I had been teaching at Pepperdine School of Law for a decade, and it turns out we we're pretty good at it. We asked if we could have our own law school with one student—Aaron. It was like we had done a Jedi thing because they said yes.

For the next four years, all the lawyers at our law firm took turns teaching Aaron law. We all got hoodies with the law school name on it so we looked the part. Graduation day came and we made Aaron give the valedictorian speech. He was also last in the class. But get this. Aaron took the bar exam and passed it. He was as surprised as we were when it happened. He got his finale. He didn't take the traditional path but still ended up at his intended destination. He stopped waiting for permission; he jumped at an opportunity.

Here's why I'm telling you these things. The world has been telling you there are only a few ways to achieve your ambitions, but that's simply not true. Comparing your path to someone else's or assuming you have to do it the way someone else did it will rob you of a great adventure. If you want to find more purpose in your life, if you're looking to find your own ambitions, help others find the path forward with their ambitions. Do this without comparison or getting lost in their ambitions and buckle up for a terrific ride.

∽

Okay, hard pivot. So far we've spent some time talking about our ambitions, how to advance them, and what gets in the way. It's time to drill down on the things we're going to need to do to move the needle on our dreams.

Part 2

SET ABSURD
EXPECTATIONS

Chapter 14

GATHER YOUR LEAVES

People who achieve their ambitions get specific about them.

S weet Maria and I had the chance to be in the Appalachian Mountains one fall with some dear friends a few weeks before Thanksgiving. As we drove to the area, every hill we crested revealed a new vista swirling with oranges, yellows, and reds as the trees transitioned into winter. We live in Southern California where we have a lot of palm trees. If you want some fronds for Palm Sunday, we've got you covered, but we're a little light on leaves because we're a little thin on colorful trees. On this trip, the fall foliage was wonderfully foreign to us, and we were soaking it all in. Sweet Maria and I were like a small crowd watching fireworks go off with oohs and aahs every time we rounded a turn in the road and more colors exploded into the sky.

We got to our destination and spent a day getting settled and enjoying the views. One of Sweet Maria's ambitions is to make people feel welcome. Among the many ways she does this is to set a beautiful and inviting table for a meal. She does this incredibly well, and her love for people is a wonderful reminder that our ambitions don't need to be loud, remote, scaled, or covered by the evening news. God delights in what He creates, and He doesn't grade our ambitions on a curve. Some ambitions can be quiet, deep, and rich; their only audience may be the person sitting across the table from us.

Since we were in the mountains, Sweet Maria asked if I could collect some of the brightly colored leaves for our Thanksgiving table. I grabbed a basket and said, "I'm the guy for the job!" I mean, how hard could it be to put some leaves in a basket? They're not that heavy.

I walked outside, my feet crunching fallen leaves as I looked for the most vibrant colors with perfect shapes. Thirty minutes later, Sweet Maria came to check on my progress. She walked up beside me, and we both looked in my basket, which was still completely empty. I hadn't grabbed a single leaf. The reason? There were just so many leaves to choose from that I didn't know which ones to pick.

Picking an ambition can be the same. There are so many to choose from that we can get paralyzed. Sometimes it's hard to know where to begin. If this sounds like you, pause and ask yourself which of your ambitions is more beautiful and lasting and impactful than all the others. This is going to take some discernment. It's like walking into a terrific bakery with racks filled with options. The truth is, when it all looks good, sometimes it's hard to pick. But if you want an ambition to move toward, it often requires picking a couple of things and deciding you're going to pursue them rather than admiring everything and doing nothing.

The corollary is equally true. Sometimes we've filled our basket to overflowing and there's simply no room for even the best addition. Maybe you've picked up and started on so many ambitions it's hard to see any of them clearly. Here's a question worth asking: are the new ambitions you're collecting every day better ambitions or just more of them?

Our lives aren't lived by chance, and we don't need to act like our ambitions are beyond our control. You have far more agency over your ambitions than you might realize. Too many people decide what ambitions they'll pursue like they are looking for answers to appear on the bottom of a Magic 8-Ball. You'll need immense creativity to dream up worthwhile ambitions; you'll need even more strategy to execute on a couple of them. Wishful thinking for a happy outcome isn't a strategy; it's deferral. Admiring the leaves isn't the same as picking a couple. If you want to see your ambitions soar, get a couple of leaves in your basket; don't just stand there looking at them.

The centerpiece of achieving your ambitions includes two crucial parts. First, we *identify* the ambition. Second, we *vet* the ambition. It's this simple and this hard.

For now we're going to focus on the identifying part. (We'll get to the vetting piece in the next chapter.) You've already collected some of your ambitions in an earlier chapter as a way to prime the pump. It's time to revisit your list and build it out some more. Sometimes if you don't write down a great thought, idea, or ambition, you'll lose it. It's like a bad dog who runs across the field and over the hill. You can whistle later all you want—but it's long gone. Don't trust your memory. It's like a flakey friend who won't be there when you really need them.

A good place to start when collecting your thoughts is to spend some serious time considering what your unexecuted ambitions have been in the past. Ask yourself why they're still on deck and why they've been either resisted or ignored. You already know where you want to go. Line up your dreams with that destination. It's easy to feel like your ambitions are staring back at you with a surprised and dazed look like a dead fish at the seafood market. It's like they can't figure out how they ended up on a bed of crushed ice. Know what you want and how you're going to get there.

You may have collected such a big pile of fall leaves that it's hard to know which one to start with. That's totally fine. It's a great place to be—full of endless possibility. Don't let your head blow up. I have one simple instruction to give you: write it all down. This is how you'll sort the leaves. Look in every nook and cranny of your past, every little whim. Pay attention to the things you keep looping back to. *I want to be a missionary. I want to hike the Pacific Crest Trail. I want to learn French. I want to visit Fiji. I want to ride an ostrich.* Write down why you want these things and which of your overarching purposes these ambitions will serve.

Don't put a big filter on what you write down. Truly, anything and everything belongs on your list at first, so long as it's coming from you. Ask friends and family you trust to remind you about what you've said to them in the past. Look at old journals from high school or college when you were less encumbered by the weight of everyday life. Pray and ask God to show you the way forward if you're unclear about it. Throw a couple of ideas His way and see how the Spirit of God, who Jesus said would be a comforter and counselor, is there for you.

If you want a way to jump-start your ideas, do the things that Jesus said really mattered to Him. Start with hungry people, then move on to thirsty people, sick people, strange people, naked people, and people in jail. You won't always know when someone is hungry, but they are everywhere. Naked people are a little more scarce, but you'll know when you've found them. Add widows and orphans if you have the opportunity. God's list for you might be longer, but I promise it won't be any shorter.

Let's get super practical. Grab your list and add every ambition you can think of. As you compile your big list, remember that they all don't need to be big and noble and noteworthy. Here are a few things that have made my initial list: visit all seven continents, learn to fly, become the lead guitarist in a band, spend the night on an aircraft carrier, raise a duck, cultivate an amazing community, put down my cell phone for a month, remove my own tonsils, restore a classic car, learn to play the cello, lose twenty-five pounds, wrestle an alligator, live without spending money for a month, climb Kilimanjaro, run a marathon, own a company, change the way people engage questions of faith, write a song, stand in the Oval Office, sleep under a bridge, save one life, help end a war, get tased, learn how to hot-wire a car, pick a lock, pilot a plane around the world, and create a new national holiday. Okay, I'm still debating about the tonsils one, but for the time being, it's staying on there.

You'll notice that the items on my list are very specific. I guess I could have gone deeper with the size of alligator I wanted to wrestle (definitely small enough so I can keep it in a headlock). Be just as specific as you can when you write down your unvetted list of ambitions, then drill down on them.

Let's say one of your ambitions is to lead a happy and fulfilling life. Most people would say the same, including me. But if you want to set yourself up to make some headway toward this beautiful ambition, you'll need to get more specific. Ask yourself what would make you feel happy and fulfilled. Would getting a puppy do the trick? How about two? Do you want to win a million dollars? Sign me up. Or would you feel even happier and more fulfilled giving away two million dollars? Sign me up for that one too. Do you want to be famous? If so, how famous and famous to whom? Do you want to be rich in friendships or in your retirement account? And how will you know when you're famous or rich enough? Figure out your metrics. Do you want your picture on a box of cereal? On a custom Nike shoe? On a wanted poster at the post office? Or would a small picture in your beloved's wallet be enough?

Get real while you're getting specific. This is what people who achieve their ambitions do. Don't write down something big and awesome and noble that you don't actually want but think you should say. Keep it real. Don't aim for just "be generous." Write down a specific and vivid example of what "being generous" looks like for you. Do you mean generous in spirit? If so, how so? You might write down "hug six old people every day" or "drop off a pie at my neighbor's house once a month." Ending world hunger would be incredible, but how about "open a food pantry across the street in my neighborhood" or "share my lunch with someone at work who looks hungry"? You won't win a Nobel Prize with that answer, but you know what? Fewer people will be hungry, and that's the point, right?

Be careful not to let limiting beliefs tell you lies about what "truly realistic" means (more on this later). If your ambition can only happen if you break the laws of physics, that would be truly unrealistic. Just because it's hard or unlikely, however, doesn't make it unrealistic. For instance, let's say you want to be able to fly. The thing about gravity is—it's a thing. Nevertheless, the Frenchman who invented a single-person jet pack came up with a work-around for the limitation of gravity. When they have them for sale on Amazon, I'm buying a couple. If you'd prefer to fly down rather than up, you could try a wingsuit. Another Frenchman invented one in 1905. He jumped off of the Eiffel Tower with it and, sadly, cratered. There wasn't a limiting belief to blame, just bad engineering. Eighty years later, someone else figured it out and lived. Go for that wingsuit. You'll look terrific at parties, at your kid's soccer games, and at the grocery store. If you get pulled over for speeding, I promise you won't get a ticket.

Filling up the basket with ambitions is one of my favorite parts of the Dream Big process. It's just how I'm wired. My hope for you is that filling your basket also fills up your heart with hope, optimism, energy, and vision for your future. If you're like me, when you look at your list, you get goose bumps and want to do a thousand push-ups and give high fives to everyone within a square mile. That's the point! When you start to acknowledge and name the ambitions that are rumbling around inside you, they open up a new vista of what life was meant to be—full of passion and purpose. Your list is a blue ocean of possibilities. Now we need to figure out what you're going to do next.

Chapter 15

SIZING UP

You can't achieve an ambition
without choosing it first.

In high school, I had two ambitions. I wanted to have one hundred dollars in the bank someday and I wanted to find a date for the prom. These were ambitious goals because I was totally broke and had never been on a date, nor were there any likely prospects. Somehow I busted the one-hundred-dollar glass ceiling by selling hotdogs downtown after school. The same week, Paula said she'd go to the prom. I was on a roll. I was living the dream. I was unstoppable. I had money and a date, and I was certain white doves would fly out of my car when I arrived at the prom with Paula and all that cash.

I spent the one hundred dollars I had renting a tuxedo, and with the little bit of cash I had left, I went in with another guy on renting a limo—with dove cages. Two days before the prom, Paula got a better invitation from a guy who was more dashing than me, which was every living eighteen-year-old male and a few sixteen-year-olds. She didn't call me "Spot" like my bully, but I guess she wasn't really into dancing with a guy who had giraffes drawn in Sharpie on his arms. She told me she wouldn't be going to the prom with me after all, and I was devastated.

There I was. No money, no date, a tux, half a limo, and a bunch of white doves I couldn't use unless I pan-fried them. I skipped the dance but learned a great life lesson about the things I was aiming for. This is what happens when it turns out that some of our ambitions either aren't worthwhile or aren't lasting. Even if I'd ended up with the cash and Paula, it doesn't mean this was the kind of beautiful, large, lasting ambition that was worth pursuing. Whether it was a relationship or a job or something else, I decided to stop wanting things that didn't want me back.

I didn't have the tools to vet my ambition when I was younger, and that lack of discernment cost me something, but it also taught me an important lesson on how to choose a worthwhile ambition. That's what vetting is all about, and that's where we're going next.

﹏

Finding your genuine, lasting ambitions is not an easy task. If it were, you'd have already accomplished it. It requires asking the questions *What do you care about? What are you willing to risk everything for?* and *Why are you so afraid?* All at the same time. It's going to take some digging and sorting and thinking and rethinking. But the effort is worth it, because when you figure out what lights you up and will outlast your other ambitions, this will inform most of your next steps. Trust me when I say the answer probably won't come the way you want it to—all downloaded in a nice and clean package without any rough edges or hard chapters. God often wraps His presents like a guy did it. (Guys, it's okay—we know most of us are bad at this.) The ambitions worth pursuing usually come a little crumpled and Scotch-taped together at first. Don't let this vetting process bum you out; let it spur you on and steel your resolve to do what it takes to get after your beautiful ambitions.

When you're vetting your ambitions, you'll likely end up with a number of possibilities in a range of sizes and difficulties. Let's say your dreams come in three sizes: easy, kind of hard, and seemingly impossible. The size of your ambitions doesn't necessary indicate the difficulty of achieving them. Think instead of the magnitude of the impact they'll have on your life and the lives of the people around you. Small ambitions can be things we're just curious about. These will stretch us personally, physically, intellectually, or relationally. They may not be laden with the kind of purpose that defines the arc of our lives. For now, they're just something fun and worth the effort to accomplish.

For example, I wanted to learn how to skydive, so I took lessons for a couple of weeks and got my license. It took me half a second to jump out of the plane. If the parachute didn't open, the jump would have taken about a minute to complete. Whether it was a good or bad ending, the ambition would have been accomplished pretty quickly. The hallmark of easy ambitions is that they can often be promptly achieved. It's helpful to have some ambitions on this smaller, easier scale because they'll invigorate you and give you the momentum you'll need to carry you toward the harder stuff. These things will also fan the flames of your other desires and make you spring out of bed in the morning. Small ambitions can sometimes lead to larger ones.

Take my friend Scott Hamilton, the former Olympic ice-skater. Adopted as a child, he had the kind of hard goal of landing a backflip on the ice. This morphed into a larger ambition to win gold at the Olympics, which changed into a huge ambition to raise a family of four, which led to the gigantic ambition to adopt two more beautiful Haitian children, all while taking on the seemingly impossible, monster ambition of beating back brain cancer with joy and a stick while raising awareness around the world about cures. And you know what? He's doing it.

Don't confuse small ambitions with tasks or tasks with small ambitions. For most people, taking out the trash is a task. It's something we do Monday morning early, before the garbage truck comes. For others, what can seem like a task to one can represent a beautiful ambition to another. I'll give you an example. On Monday mornings, my neighbor Pat would get up early and take his trash out. This would be a task for most of us. He didn't stop there. He took out his neighbors' trash cans too. I know this because I was one of those neighbors. Why did he do this? This activity wasn't merely a task for Pat. It was the expression of a beautiful ambition he had to love his neighbors the way Jesus said to. He didn't want to go across the ocean to do it, so he walked across the street. Pat was actually a really successful restauranteur across North America, but taking out my trash was just as important to him. What more practical way was there to love the people who lived near him than to take out their garbage cans? It was genius. Something small was anything but a task for Pat; it was the fulfillment of a huge and noble and worthwhile ambition of his. What's yours?

I've had a couple of medium-sized, kind-of-difficult ambitions too. These were things that were going to take some additional effort. I feel older than dirt when I say this, but we've put on a parade as a family in our neighborhood every year for more than a quarter of a century. Hundreds of people turn out each year, and it takes our family more than a couple of minutes to organize and pull it off, as you would imagine. We do this because we crave community and want to celebrate doing life with our neighbors. The task of inflating thousands of helium balloons in our living room at 4:00 a.m. for our parade is actually feeding into a bigger, larger, and more lasting dream of doing this together as a family, which serves an even bigger ambition of celebrating our neighbors and friends. When we get tired of tying the tiny ends of the balloons, we remind ourselves *why* we do it. You'll need to remind yourself too. Tasks aren't always merely tasks; they can be stepping-stones.

Large and seemingly impossible ambitions are going to require equally large sacrifices. They're not going to be achieved easily or quickly, so don't fool yourself into thinking you'll stumble upon them some day. Do you want to repair the environment? Fix your marriage? Get a master's degree? End a war? These are beautiful and seemingly impossible ambitions, but I hope you'll pursue these if your heart is bending toward them.

We've been working in the Islamic Republic of Afghanistan for the last couple of years. The Taliban won't let young girls learn how to read and write for one reason: they are girls. We started a school in the former capital of the Taliban and teach young boys and girls alike how to read and write and have the life skills they will need to lead their country someday. This was a big, seemingly impossible ambition and has involved some significant risks and sacrifices. Your big ambitions may exact a high price as well. Don't expect your biggest ambitions to walk into the room like a puppy and lie down by the fire. These ambitions *are* the fire.

〜

Here are a few things you can think about when sizing up an ambition to pursue.

Is your ambition meaningful? Stated differently, *Is it worthwhile and lasting?* Don't busy yourself with things that merely occupy your time. We all pick our vice. Is television or golf or Netflix robbing you of your time? These can be great ways to relax, but they might not be great paths toward your ambitions. Are you catching up on everyone else's lives on social media, or are you exploring and expanding yours? Only you will know the answers. I'm not suggesting what your ambition should be. I'm advocating that you ask the questions and find answers that launch you forward toward the best of them.

"Try on" your ambition. Some people try to sprint before they've thought things through or even heard the starting pistol fire. Others hear the gun but spend too much time thinking about how long the race is or what shoes they're wearing that they never take a step forward. There's a middle way. You can "try on" your ambition as you decide whether it's worth the time and sacrifice required to make it happen. Don't buy the house; rent the home. Take your ambitions out on dates. Go to the park together and touch knees. Walk on the beach with your ambitions and hold hands. Take them on a drive around the block. Compare one of your time-consuming ambitions to another one and go with the best one. Discern whether the impediments that seem to be in the way of your ambitions are based in reality or fear. Ask yourself if your ambition lines up with something God said He valued for our lives. Remember, your ambition will only have value to you if you give it space in your life. If you're not willing to try it on first, maybe it's not worth pursuing.

Will it last? The ambitions worth pursuing are those with the longest shelf life. Get clear about what you believe will last in your life. Pro tip here: the convertible Jag won't. You'll look like a boss for a while, but soon you're just another person stuck in traffic. Being famous probably won't last either unless you're Santa or Tom Hanks. Stress test your ambition. Will it matter in a year? Ten years? How about in one hundred years? I'll be honest with you and admit the sad truth about many of my early ambitions—they started with a shiny luster, but they tarnished faster than a copper penny in salt water.

Is it all about you or will it help others? One problem that has tended to get in the way of my ambitions is that I've made everything about myself. Perhaps you have too. I'm aware of how I feel, I know what I want, and I know what I think. This kind of self-awareness is helpful, to be sure, but only when it's coupled with a greater amount of other-awareness. How do the people around me feel? What do they want, and what do they think? Ambitions that are only for you are not inherently bad; they just lack the right mix of richness and depth and "otherness." They are part of the picture, but they're just a pixel, not even close to the whole image. Make sure you set your compass in the right direction: always pointing toward the things that will last and make an impact in the lives of others. You'll know you're moving toward beautiful ambitions in your life if you find yourself wanting beautiful things for the people around you. Your greatest sense of fulfillment will come in the service of others, not yourself. Don't fall for the idea that pursuing your ambitions and helping others is a binary choice. You don't need to choose between ambitions that help others or inspire you. Find things that do both at the same time. You'll be more energized and grateful, and as a result you'll throw more of your life into it.

What do you want to be remembered for? Another way to vet your list is to think about what kind of legacy you want to leave behind. Thinking about what will be said at your funeral feels like a too predictable (and sobering) way to make sure your life leads to a few beautiful words. What about envisioning how your ambition gets talked about at the water cooler at work?

Is it possible? Don't discard an ambition because it seems too hard or is seemingly impossible. There's a difference between "my ambition isn't realistic" and "I'm afraid to try" or "this will be really hard." Don't let the scale of your ambitions head-fake you into abandoning them. Stated differently, don't let your ideas sink at the dock because you were afraid to untie them and set sail across an ocean. At the same time, acknowledge when a worthwhile ambition has morphed into a crazy pipedream. Here's an example from my list. I'd love to be an astronaut and go to the moon, so I wrote it down. The reality, though, is that unless I come to own SpaceX, it's not going to happen. I could buy a share of stock someday if Elon Musk does an IPO. But for me, going to the moon probably doesn't pass the test of *Is it possible?* At least for now.

～

Do your ambitions live up to your abilities, attributes, desires, and willingness to act? Do the arrows point from your gifting toward your ambitions, or are they completely unrelated? Your abilities are unique to you; they're a mixture of how God made you and the life experiences you've had up to this point. Does your ambition at least feel adjacent to things you already know or have experienced or can learn?

I'll give you an example. If you're four feet nine inches tall and forty-five years old, does "become an NBA basketball star" seem like a good fit for your abilities and attributes? If we're being honest, probably not. Okay, that's too generous. Heck no, not even close. Put a hoop up on the garage at your house and practice your dunk, but you're not going to be getting on a professional basketball court on game day anytime soon. You might have all the desire and willingness in the world, but that won't change your bone structure or age.

～

For as long as I can remember, I had an ambition to have a place where people could gather, find rest, and go deeper in their relationships with God and each other. Over the course of twenty years, we built the Lodge I've mentioned. Then some workers made a mistake and it burned down in twenty minutes. That'll preach. All of our efforts were reduced to a pile of ashes and melted glass. The memories we made there floated into the sky and disappeared into the clouds. We've all suffered loss. It may not have been your home that burned down, but maybe it was a relationship or a career or a hope.

It took us a year to grieve the loss and another four to rebuild the Lodge. That's almost twenty-five years of pursuing the same ambition. Why would I spend most of my adult life pursuing this? It's simple. I believed from the beginning that it would be absolutely worth it. I believed this ambition would be an expression of what's most important to me: a place for my family to connect, serve others, find true rest, and invite people into an adventure with Jesus that is drenched in love.

Think about your own ambitions. Among the many things you may have written down, which of them would you spend twenty or more years making a reality? Then, stress test your idea. If it all turned to ashes, would you rebuild it all over again? That's the kind of resolve and intent I'm talking about. You'll know you're on the scent of a worthwhile, lasting ambition when the strong scent of a smoldering fire wouldn't dampen your resolve to build it twice even before you had built it for the first time.

Chapter 16

GET THE STICKS
BEFORE THE DRUMS

It doesn't matter what your ambition
looks like; it matters what it is.

Too many people let the improbability of their ambitions keep them from taking to the air. One way to give an ambition some lift is to couple it with one of your already existing ambitions. I did this with the Lodge and my desire to learn how to fly. Learning how to fly had been ambition of mine for years. I wedded this to my existing ambition of having a safe place in a remote location, where people could meet and have meaningful conversations. Combined, these ambitions pointed toward a possibility. I was already a lawyer (also an ambition). I knew how to start things and do the legal wrangling necessary, so a friend and I applied to start an airline in Canada. I know it sounds ridiculous, but I'm not kidding. We let one ambition serve the next ambition, which in turn served the next ambition and the next. Get the picture?

We decided to call the airline "Pacific Wings" because it sounded cool and aeronautical. We found out a year later there was already an airline with the same name in Hawaii, flying jets between the islands. We assumed they'd change their name and repaint their planes if they had a problem with our airline.

We got through the entire process, except for one thing. We didn't own an airplane, and I couldn't afford one. Remember this: people who get things done don't let impediments have the last say. They find workarounds. They'll spin the building if that's what it takes and make the back door look like the front door.

The thing about seaplanes is they hit stuff. There were 1,657 Beavers built, but a whole lot less of them exist now. That means people are constantly trying to find buyers for the pieces of their planes they could salvage. We started buying seaplane parts as they came up for sale. We got the wings from one guy who was still a little bruised up, the fuselage from another, and the floats from someone else. Home Depot supplied the duct tape. We needed to give the plane a new paint job to cover up all the welding. I was in Krispy Kreme getting donuts, not for me but for this friend of mine, when I saw the colors on the box. I knew we had our colors. We didn't even try to be discreet about it—we used all of them. The green, the white, the red, the font. Everything but the glazing on the donuts. The plane looked like a flying box of diabetes.

We had our airline and we had one cobbled-together airplane. Unfortunately every time we started the engine, it was like throwing hundred-dollar bills into the propeller. Sure, we'd get the odd passenger or two, but it cost far more to operate the plane than we were making by selling tickets. We could have packed it in and gone out of business, but we didn't. Worthwhile ambitions, when they've been vetted, have staying power. We didn't quit; we adapted. We started flying into every logging camp up every inlet each day with newspapers and fresh vegetables. Within a year, we owned six Beavers and two other wheel planes. Here's the point. Find several of your ambitions and see if one can serve another. Just because one ambition seems improbable, don't leave it grounded on the tarmac. If things get tough, remember why you started and stay at it. Give your idea a quarter twist. If it doesn't seem like you can afford your ambition, get on Craigslist and start buying it a piece at a time.

I think I'd make a lousy evangelist. Here's why: I don't want to be an advertisement for Jesus; I'd rather be proof. A recent study concluded that each of us is exposed to at least five thousand advertisements each day telling us what we want. No wonder we're confused. When you're writing down your ambitions and winnowing the list to what's worth the pursuit, don't worry about whether your dreams seem cool or flashy or religious or evangelical enough. People fall into this trap all the time. Appearances are a house of mirrors. They distort reality. They'll make your ambitions look thinner or fatter or more unreasonable and twisted than they really are. The same is true about appearances if faith guides you. Don't waste your time worrying about what will make you look good or pious or holy. Take action because you're able to and because you believe that God is good and all that really matters is that you're His. Simply put, if it matters more what your faith looks like than what it is, it's time to start all over again.

Not long ago, I had an ambition to learn how to play the drums. I had seen a guy onstage at an event and he was sitting behind a huge set of fire-engine-red drums. He had about a dozen cymbals on stands around him and seemed to be hitting all the drums and cymbals at the same time. It was like he had three arms. I wanted to be like that guy for one reason. He looked like a boss.

The next weekend, I jumped in my pickup truck and headed to the local music store. They had rooms full of instruments, and I walked into the one where they kept all the drum sets. There were probably a hundred sets of drums displayed on the wall. My head swiveled back and forth like it was on ball bearings to take in the drum sets for sale. I wanted all of them. It didn't take long for me to zero in on a fire-engine-red setup on the top row like the ones I had seen earlier. I was going to look like a boss too. Maybe I'd get a new haircut and a tattoo on my face. I wasn't sure. But maybe.

I didn't say a word to the salesman as he walked up. I just stood there pointing at the red drums. We both knew what I meant. We also both knew I'm too old to be cool and couldn't pull it off if I wanted to. The earlier version of me would have thrown my credit card on the counter anyway and started loading the drums into the back of my truck. But, standing in the store, I realized something was changing about the way I was pursuing my ambitions.

I walked out of the music store that day with a six-dollar set of drumsticks. Do you know why? Instead of *looking* like a boss, I decided I wanted to *play* like a boss. It was going to take a lot of lessons and hard work, so I decided to take a small step first. The same will be true of your worthwhile ambitions. If we're going to get serious about pursuing them, we need to stop caring about what our lives look like to everyone else and instead care about what they actually are. If you come over to my house now, you'll see I have pots and pans set up in the living room. They're not much to look at to most people, but they all look fire-engine red to me.

Don't allow the impediments you encounter throw you off the scent. I have a friend named Al who wanted to be a philanthropist. The problem was that he didn't have any money. He could have bailed on his ambition, but he's not that kind of person, and you aren't either.

To advance his ambition to give away money, he wrote a terrific book called *The Boy, the Kite, and the Wind*. It's a beautiful story, and every copy sold fills his philanthropy fund so he can give more money away. He calls himself the "improbable philanthropist" these days. Indeed, Al. Improbable? Perhaps. Effective? Totally. His life has inspired thousands to lead more generous and engaged lives—and I'm one of them.

As I look back over my life, it seems I usually get some of the things I've wanted and an equal number of things I didn't want. Some of my ambitions were easy to achieve and others weren't. I haven't installed a circuit breaker to shut down the improbable ambitions when the results of my efforts have looked uncertain. Instead, I give myself license to pursue all the available opportunities I can find. The nature of my ambitions has changed as well. It's not material things—like a set of drums—I want these days; it's relationships, building schools in other countries, and, with a spirit of kindness, engaging people I find difficult to get along with.

As you marshal your ambitions, don't rush the process. Take as long as you need. For some, this is an hour; for others it could take a month. Do it at your pace. Some people get clarity on their ambitions waiting in the drive-through line; others go on a weekend retreat. Do whatever works for you, whatever helps you populate your collection of desires that are true and lasting. Find ambitions that will positively impact the lives of others and get you fired up to pursue a few more ambitions for yourself. If you're going to spend your time, talent, and treasure to get some of those dreams off the ground, isn't it worth the investment of time and conviction to find the right ones?

It's fun to sit and daydream, but if that's all we do, we're not really on the path to accomplishing anything. Like I said earlier, when you get all the leaves in one place and start sorting through them, you're going to find the standouts. Do the deep work in your life so the right ones catch your eye. I promise you're going to like what you see.

Part 3

EXPLORE OPPORTUNITIES

Chapter 17

KEEP THE MOON IN THE WINDOW

The path to your ambitions isn't linear;
keep moving toward them.

I received a call not long ago from a young man who asked me, "What's the one thing about relationships?" With a chuckle, I said, "You haven't had a girlfriend yet, have you?" It would be like asking an astronaut, "What's the *one thing* about getting to the moon?" I bet she would shrug and say, "I don't know . . . arrive?"

Seriously, if I wanted to get to the moon, here's what I'd do. I'd find someone who had built plenty of rocket ships before and had successfully launched a couple. I'm certain I wouldn't spend any time with people who wanted to argue about what color to paint the booster. I'd also be really picky about who I'd let get in the capsule with me and even more picky about who I'd let speak into my ear. You should be too. The final important thing I'd do if I wanted to get to the moon is this: I'd keep the moon in the window and keep pointing in its direction. Forget having Jesus take the wheel. Get Him in the window and keep pointing at Him. It's going to take a thousand mid-course corrections to get to the moon, and it will take at least the same amount of course corrections to arrive at your ambitions. Don't be fooled into thinking your ambition is about figuring out the "one thing" you need to do to get there. Look for an opportunity to keep moving forward, and find some people you trust who have launched more things into the world than you have. Ask for help. They'll probably help you start the ignition sequence on your ambitions.

When I am clear on my ambitions, it feels like I'm handling enriched uranium, without the whole axis of evil thing. It feels powerful and dangerous. I get excited by the possibilities and envision what it would be like when one of my ambitions explodes into the world, releasing love, hope, and inspiration into the lives of those around me. Do you have one of these you've kept below the decks in your life? It's tired of waiting.

From this point forward, we're going to figure out how to put wheels on the bus. It's not an easy thing to move your dream into reality. But it's not a terribly mystical process either. You can do it, step by step, on-ramp by on-ramp. The path to getting there is to explore opportunities and see how you can navigate toward your ambitions.

Ditch the desire for instant gratification. Celebrate every small piece of progress, even if there are nine hundred and ninety-nine more things to do. If you're the kind of person who gets jittery only thinking and dreaming, this is where the process starts to get *real*.

As you embark on this journey, it's tempting to want it all mapped out. But life doesn't tend to follow our plans. Instead, we need to think of exploring opportunities as following a trail of breadcrumbs. With each move you make, you'll start to notice momentum building in one direction and not in another. This is normal. You can't go down every path at once. Exploring opportunities will give you the confidence to know you're on the right trail. Also, it may be that this step will lead you exactly to your ambition. It doesn't happen often, but it's possible. Let me give you a couple of examples of how I explored a few opportunities.

I knew I was going to be in London to speak at a conference held each year in a huge arena. I knew the date I would arrive in May, so I wrote the queen of England. Her address isn't hard to find: Buckingham Palace, London, SW1A 1AA. Address your letters to the queen. You don't need her first name. They'll know who you're talking about.

In my note to the queen, I simply said, "I'm going to be in London on May 14. If you're in London on May 14, let's meet." A week later, I received a reply on Buckingham Palace letterhead. It was from one of her ladies in waiting. I thought to myself, *Lady, what are you waiting for?* She said the queen was terribly disappointed she couldn't meet with me. I'm sure it tore her up.

I could have been home watching *Stranger Things* or playing Candy Crush. Instead, for the price of an envelope and a dollar in postage, I was talking to Buckingham Place. You can too. I'm still waiting to have tea with the queen, but putting yourself into the stream of possibility is what it looks like to explore opportunities.

Every year I also write a letter to the pope. I ask if I can meet with him. Every year I get the same reply from somebody other than the pope, usually an assistant bishop. He always says the same thing in a word: "No." Do I think God closed the door? Not really. I just know I've still got the right address.

Just because I've received a couple of nos doesn't mean I'm going to abandon an ambition. Don't you dare stop either. No miner strikes gold with the first swing of the pick. Who knows? Maybe a hole will open up in the pope's schedule. Same for the queen. Maybe I'll get us all together. Perhaps I need to buy a plane ticket to Rome and sit outside his front door to see if I can get in. Or maybe I should apply to join the queen's guard. I can't lie; I could rock a bear-skin hat. I'm not talking about stalking people, but I am talking about going for it. People who have big ambitions pursue even the smallest opportunities everywhere. The more outlandish and unlikely, the better.

Exploring opportunities takes a little bit of focused intentionality. Is this person I met a part of the journey? That article looks like it might have some ideas for me. I sense I need to attend that new church for a few Sundays. These are the types of breadcrumb trails people follow when they're on the scent of their big dreams.

⌇

I love In-N-Out Burger. If you haven't been there, you haven't lived—you're just existing. I was thirteen when I tasted a Double-Double and knew there was a God. Ryan is a friend of mine from high school. He got a job at an In-N-Out Burger and it felt to me like he had somehow found the cheat codes for the entire game of life. He was on fries and wearing a red apron when I dropped by. This was the job I wanted, but it wasn't the job he wanted. He had other ambitions and wanted to explore all the opportunities available to him. After a couple of other jobs, one of which he worked at for free, he saw a tweet from a startup company looking for help and asking for tips on how to get started. Ryan's Twitter reply was simple: "Here's a tip. Email me."

The startup company was called Uber, and Ryan became one of the first employees. Eventually he became the CEO of the company. This is both amazing and well deserved. Ryan saw an opportunity and went for it. These days, he has a new ambition that is even bigger and bolder. He wants to continue being a great husband and father to his wife and kids. He quit his job at Uber, moved away with the family, and is investing deeply and courageously in them. He's treating his family like his second startup and he's throwing everything he's got at it. Ryan saw an opportunity and seized it. You can too. This never would've happened if Ryan wasn't paying attention to the opportunities around him and ready to make the moves he needed when they came his way.

Don't keep your ideas stuck in your head. Don't get stuck at the fry station either. It's honorable work, but it might not be your only work. People who are ready to go after their ambitions are constantly on the lookout for opportunities. They don't see obstacles; they see possibilities. Making moves is catnip for them. They've learned what seems to be a law of the universe: one opportunity leads to the next one, and the next, and the next. Pretty soon they have a daisy chain of little wins that ultimately leads to their bigger, more impossible ambitions. Opportunities always find the people who are looking for them the most.

People who are looking for opportunities usually find them because they're willing to spend enough dedicated time looking for them. "Somewhere Over the Rainbow" is great song, but it's a lousy way to pursue your ambitions.

༄

A real practical way to get some quick momentum on your ambition is research. I know it sounds boring, but it won't be. You'll be lapping up Google searches, I promise. Do you want to start a nonprofit but have no idea where to begin? Some research will give you the answers. Do you need to explain the fiscal impact of your ambitions to give to investors, except you've never put together a profit-and-loss statement? Do a little research. Do you have talents wasting away in the wrong job but know deep down there's a better use for them? Research it.

As you prepare to make some moves and tune your life into your ambitions, get to know some of the names in your desired space. Figure out how to contact them via email and send them a message. Follow them on social media and join the conversation. Set a Google alert and you'll receive an email every time the person comes up in the news. It's like non-creepy stalking. Attend conferences and be polite, but muscle your way to the front of the line. Introduce yourself to people.

This is what it looks like to be prepared. Get ready now, not later. Do your homework. Be on the lookout for when the opportunity comes. Keep your eyes open. Stay engaged. People committed to their ambitions don't wait for doors to open. They knock, then they ring the doorbell, then they camp out. They remain incredibly attentive and respectful while assuming they are invited to their ambitions rather than waiting endlessly for permission.

Chapter 18

THE NUMBER FOR THE WHITE HOUSE IS (202) 456-1414

Make the call and know what to say.

When my son Adam was young, six or seven years old, we were driving in my pickup truck. Adam is usually a really upbeat and happy kid, but this day he was feeling pretty sick. Maybe it was a cold, or perhaps the flu—we weren't quite sure. Like me, when Adam gets sick, he gets very quiet and more than a little melancholy. So I said to him in my cheeriest voice, "Hey, Adam, we need to tell President Bush that you're feeling lousy. Let's call him."

"Huh?" Adam grunted and glanced up and gave me one of those *Dad, you're nuts* looks.

I started dialing. The phone number for the White House is (202) 456-1414. Write it down. I don't care if you like the one living on Pennsylvania Avenue when you read this or not. Presidents change, but the White House phone number doesn't.

I put the call on the speaker of my cell phone. Adam was still totally out of it and curled up in the fetal position in the passenger seat. After a few rings, a pleasant and very proper executive voice came on the phone and answered, "White House." Adam was coming out of his haze as I told the nice woman that my son Adam and I were driving in my pickup truck and that Adam was terribly sick. We thought it might be a cold. We knew the president would want to know and I asked if she would either put us through to him, or if he wasn't available to speak to us right then, could she transfer us to the president's scheduling assistant so that we could set up a time to come and meet with the president so that Adam could tell him all about it.

After a short moment, the woman professionally and efficiently said, "One moment please," and put us on hold. By now Adam was starting to come around and was sitting upright in his seat. His look communicated he had upgraded me from "nuts" to "certifiably insane."

After a short hold, a new voice answered the phone, even more proper and executive than the first. "This is the president's office," the woman answered. I explained again how Adam and I were in my pickup truck and Adam was terribly sick. He had sneezed five or six times. Bare minimum. I let her know we thought we should let the president know right away. By this time, Adam wasn't sitting in the front seat of the truck anymore; he was standing on the seat, his eyes full of anticipation and amazement. His grimace had been replaced with a big grin as he listened to the conversation with total engagement.

The assistant offered that the president wasn't available to talk to us right then, but she quickly turned the conversation to Adam. "Hello, Adam?" she said in a nurturing voice. "I'm so sorry to hear that you aren't feeling well, honey, and I'll make sure I tell the president right away. Would that be okay with you?" Adam didn't say anything but nodded in agreement. Somehow, she knew. She continued, "Adam, can I ask you one question?"

"Sure," he said, leaning so far forward I thought he would fall out of the seat.

"How are you feeling now?"

Adam was still standing on the passenger seat; his eyes were clear and focused. He was flush with excitement; he was totally engaged. He was all in. And why not? He was talking to the White House! After a short pause, Adam stammered, "Well, you know, I'm feeling a little better!" putting his palm on his forehead and pulling it away to show me.

Getting engaged and pursuing opportunities isn't like playing ding-dong-ditch with God. It has nothing to do with daring God to do something. In fact, it's the opposite. Sometimes it takes a big dose of strategic whimsy and daring ourselves to take the next unlikely step to see where it leads. It's moving from the bleachers to the field. It's moving from developing opinions to developing options. It's about having things matter to us so much we are willing to overcome a couple of impediments to get to them. And what's probably the best part about this kind of engagement is that it's contagious. Once it goes viral, there's no stopping it.

Knowing who to call is where it starts, but there's something else of equal importance: know what you want to say when someone answers your call. When I called the White House, I wasn't surprised that they answered—well, maybe I was a little bit surprised. But once they answered, I needed to be ready with what it was that I wanted to say. A couple million people have my cell phone number. At least a quarter of those calls come from people who don't know what to say when I answer. I think those people wonder if it's true that I'll answer. The silence usually means people haven't made it to that part where they know what to say yet, which is fine. When I pick up the phone, you have got my undivided attention, but you're not going to have it for long if you're not prepared. Realize that I've put down or interrupted whatever I was doing to honor the time for the person calling. The same will be true of whomever you call. Do your part when you're pursuing your ambition and know what you want to say. "Is this really you?" is cute, but it's a nonstarter.

If you call someone to help you with your ambition, get to the point. Don't talk about the weather or sports or your dog. Don't be a fan; be a new friend who knows why they are calling and what they want. If you don't get what you want, don't pout about it, and don't say something snarky. Be polite and think about who your next call is going to be. The next call you need to make may end up requiring additional calls as well. Make these calls like a boss. Look—you've got the phone number for the White House. You're unstoppable.

~

There tends to be a honeymoon period when you're pursuing an ambition. The early days are fueled by newfound momentum. Life can feel so fresh when you're hot on the pursuit. But I want to warn you about putting too many lines in the water. Is it good to up your chances of hooking an opportunity? Sure. It can get messy, though, when you overextend yourself by short-circuiting any sense of pace or sequence to your actions. Think of it like multitasking. According to science, there's no such thing. Our brains are wired to focus on one thing at a time. When you try to multitask your ambitions, you're actually just doing lots of little disjointed things one at a time with very little focus.

Sure, it can look like we're doing lots of things. Maybe we think looking busy to the outside world conveys a sense of progress or accomplishment. Don't be fooled. You can spin your wheels for a week laying track only to find none of it really connects. It's okay to slow down and remember where you left off on one thing and started the next. Pick one thing at a time and throw your energy into that. Move your ambition forward as far as you can. Then move it a little further forward. Be methodical, intentional, and consistent, and you'll blow your mind with the progress you make.

There's a saying in the South: "Be where your feet are." It's a Southern way of underscoring the importance of being fully present where you are. This is difficult for some of us. Here's my suggestion: do it anyway. Be present with the tasks in front of you. Let the other things worry about themselves while you finish. With all the distractions available, it's easy to chase butterflies. You might be swinging your net wildly; you might even be snagging a few things. But when you look up, you'll probably realize you are way off the path to your ambition because you mistook quantity for quality.

To explore opportunities effectively, you must be fully present where you are. This will require some moves on your part. Lose the distractions. Break up with stress. Toss your stupid smartphone. It's not the garden of Eden, but the thing in your hand you've been talking on may be your undoing—it wouldn't be the first time an Apple did us in. The only thing instant about a message on your phone is that it will instantly highjack your attention and land you somewhere other than where you are. Protect your attention.

When it comes to your ambitions, I'm giving you permission to be incredibly picky about the work you take on. This isn't the dinner table when you were a kid; you have the agency to find something different if what's in front of you isn't something you like. Just because it's an opportunity doesn't mean it's the right one. Just because it's a job you've had in the past doesn't mean it's the job for your future. I'm not advocating for a life of indecisiveness. Quite the opposite. I want you to be so clear about what you want to see in your life that you won't confuse your important commitments for the unimportant ones. Commitments will cost you time, and you can't create more of that.

People chasing their ambitions get really good at saying no in just the right way. (I'll show you how in a little bit.)

Once you generate some next steps toward your ambitions, you're going to feel more excitement and possibility swelling up around you. Don't get off the scent if things don't turn out the way you were hoping. Don't be discouraged if you don't get a call back. Don't ditch your ambition because it will cost more money or take more time than you can imagine having. Keep on task. Tune into your life as if you're following an invisible path toward your ambition. Make sure it squares with what you believe, and then throw everything you have at it.

As people undertake all of these actions, many find that there are some barriers already in place. Maybe some past choices or current responsibilities are standing between you and the progress you need to make. To get past those barriers, it might take a hard conversation. It might take a stick of dynamite. It's up to you decide. The only choice you should take off the table is pulling a one-eighty and walking away.

Part 4

CLEAR THE PATH

Chapter 19

HOSTAGE NEGOTIATION

Figure out what's holding you back.

It was September 1973 in Stockholm, Sweden. A convicted felon left prison after serving a portion of his sentence. Think of it like probation. He was getting a second chance at life, a chance to prove he could reenter society and do it right this time. It didn't work. Soon after he was released, he headed to a bank to rob it and took four hostages when it went wrong. There was a five-day standoff before the Swedish authorities filled the bank with tear gas to flush him out.

When the robber was brought to trial, the four hostages were obviously the key witnesses. Surprisingly, following the trauma of the experience, the four hostages refused to say anything negative about the person who had held them captive for almost a week. This led to what we now call "Stockholm syndrome." Maybe you've heard of it. It's a name given to the inexplicable psychological phenomenon where a person develops affection for the person causing their affliction. Simply put, they developed a weirdly codependent relationship with their captor.

It doesn't just happen in bank robberies, though. Think about it. Who do you know who can't break the cycle of bad relationships? Do you know someone who goes through predictable cycles of addiction and can't seem to break free? What about the person obsessively checking their phone for work emails while they are supposed to be on vacation? That last one is seemingly more benign than the others, but it's not. Many of us are clinging with affection to the very things that are holding us hostage. You know I'm talking about you right now, right? It could be anything. A routine, a relationship, a job, a deeply held belief caused by a childhood wound. It might even be fair to say that we're all being held hostage by something to some degree. Some of the most important work you will do is to identify who or what has been keeping you captive and to break free. We can't fix what we don't understand.

You can't move forward with your new ambitions without sloughing off some of your old hang-ups, and we can't simply walk away from these hang-ups without understanding them first. Here's something to consider: our current failures are often an echo of our past ones. As we come to understand these cycling behaviors, we get the clues we need to figure out what's underneath the surface and holding us back. Here's the good news: you can turn whatever has been holding you hostage into a path toward freedom by understanding what that is and then breaking your relationship with it. If you want to accomplish your ambitions, you're going to have to learn some Houdini-level escape tricks. To do this you will have to clear the path of anything standing in the way.

We need to figure out what limiting beliefs we have developed that have us convinced that our ambitions are not available to us. These limiting beliefs come in all shapes and sizes for us. But they have one unifying characteristic—they hold us back. I have them and you have them. They are the invisible ghosts whispering that we'll never make it, that we can't accomplish our ambitions, that we missed our chance. I bet you've heard that voice in your head saying, *You're not smart enough* or *You're not attractive enough* or *You don't have the right gifts and talents to accomplish that* or *You missed your only chance.* These ugly, untrue messages will flood our minds if we're not on guard. Where do these voices come from? My bet is that they didn't originate with you. If you drill down on them, you'll probably find they originated with a parent or a coach, a sibling or a pastor, a teacher or a bully, an old boyfriend or girlfriend. Or maybe the voice in your head is a mashup of some or all of these.

We have a drawer at our house where we keep a box full of keys. I don't know what most of them unlock or where they came from. Like you, I didn't want to lose the ability to possibly unlock something I had, so I kept them all, not understanding which locks the keys went with. I've wondered if there were little elves in the attic hiding more of them each night. I was going to set some traps that looked like locks and see if I could catch a couple. These keys are of zero use to us, yet still we keep them because we think we might need them someday.

That box of keys is like the hang-ups in our lives. They are habits and beliefs and patterns that may have served us at one point, but don't any longer. Yet still we hang on to them thinking they might be useful later. This is how limiting beliefs operate. We don't even remember how we got them. They are of no use to us, and they don't unlock anything, but we've given them full access to our most deeply held beliefs.

We've all given more than a couple of keys away too. We've done a key exchange with people we don't even know but listen to because they are loud or authoritative or convincing. We have allowed them in and treated them like guests when they are actually trespassers in our lives. We've given keys to some of our life choices too. There's a swap happening with our careers and cars and bank accounts and retirement plans. The hard work comes when we start understanding our keys—the ones we've got, the ones we've given away, and the ones we don't need anymore.

If you want to do some detective work on your life, look at your behaviors. Are you bad at relationships? Maybe your parents got divorced so you started to believe your path would be the same. Did your parents stay up at night over a dimly lit kitchen table wondering how they could afford the electricity bill? Perhaps this is the origin of your worldview that the resources you need will be scarce. Do you remember playing musical chairs and you're afraid you'll be the one without a seat when the music stops? Maybe this is where your fear of rejection came from. Did you get made fun of for your freckles or get dumped by a prom date? These could be the return address of some of your insecurities.

Limiting beliefs can be anything, really, and they're unique to each of us. If you want to clear the path to your ambitions, you're going to have to stare down some monsters that have made their way into your closet or under your bed or into your life. You have to silence these old voices telling you lies about yesterday so the truth of today becomes a little bit more audible.

I guess what I'm saying is that none of us, literally not a single person, pursues their ambitions without having to face the moments in their past that have influenced their beliefs and deciding what they'll do about them. The only question is whether you'll stop, recognize that a limiting belief has grabbed the microphone in your life, understand what is happening, and tune out what isn't true. If you don't, there's a chance you'll let the lies you've believed in the past repeat themselves until the day you die.

Limiting beliefs can be multigenerational too. Have you ever stopped and said or done something and wondered, *Where on earth did that come from?* Because I've done some of the deep work throughout my life to identify and understand these, I know the well-worn paths to go find the starting point and bury it in the dirt. Let me give you an example.

I grew up in Northern California and liked to hike in the Sierra Nevada mountains with my dad. He has always been a bright and caring and cautious guy and would let me know about the dangers present as a way of expressing love to me. He would point to a log and tell me a cautionary tale about how rattlesnakes try to stay out of the sun by hiding under the logs. Evidently, the only way to not get bit was to stand on the top of the log then make a big leap out beyond where the snake could reach your ankles with its fangs. On its face, this seems like a good and fatherly instruction to give, and in one sense, it absolutely was. My dad wanted to help me stay safe. Because he loves me, he didn't want me to get bit by rattlesnakes, or maybe he didn't want to suck venom out of my calf if it happened. Either way, it came from a good and caring place.

I've been hiking in the Sierras for four decades, and do you know how many rattlesnakes I've seen? Zero. And that's rounding up. Even so, do you know what I do every time I get to a log? I step on top and leap as far away as I can so I don't get bit. I see a twig on the sidewalk downtown and a leap a foot or two in case a baby snake is under it.

My dad wasn't trying to mess with my head. He was trying to be helpful. Still, the warning instilled itself in my young mind as a belief that rattlesnakes are under every log. The best way to overcome the belief like this isn't to jump into a pit full of snakes; that's just stupid. It's to understand the belief and where it came from. If we don't, we'll be so busy not stepping on cracks or walking under ladders or breaking mirrors that we'll never really start living our own authentic lives.

Like me with the log and the snake, our limiting beliefs usually take the shape of fear. This can manifest as procrastination, rational- izing, busyness, and a host of other subconscious tactics we employ to keep from chasing our ambitions. Whether the fear is rational or not, it feels real. Fear boxes us in and will always try to talk us into settling for lesser things. If we let fear push us around, it won't be long before we're all fences and no horses. If you want to clear the path toward your ambitions, you need to figure out what you're afraid of and why you're afraid of it.

Here's a hard truth you need to understand as you pinpoint your fears: they will not go away by themselves. They're more likely to multiply like rabbits in the dark. Listen up. Fears don't really get fully conquered; they're just understood and given less power. Be strong and courageous. Understand what fears are driving you. Are you willing to slay the dragon to move toward your ambition? Figure out your fears, kick them in the teeth, and get back to work. You're not a hostage anymore.

Chapter 20

GIVE IT A QUARTER TWIST

We discover and build our
ambitions in installments.

Thankfully there's an opposite to limiting beliefs, and it can often come from the same family tree (just different branches). I call these launching beliefs. My grandparents on my mom's side were kind, generous with their time, and deeply loving. My grandfather was a fireman on the wharf in the San Francisco Bay. He worked the graveyard shift for forty years, but he never put out a fire. I don't even know if he knew how to. But he and my grandmother were great at loving me. They made it their purpose. From my young perspective, it seemed like it was the one thing, above all things, that mattered to them.

My grandparents lived a few miles from my house when I was growing up. I had a room in their house they set aside just for me. There was a small drawer in the room, and my grandparents would fill it full of nickels. They called it "room rent" and put a nickel in each time they came into my room. This delighted me. It wasn't the cash that lit me up; it was about honor and acknowledgement. The thought that I mattered so much my grandparents would keep track of the times when they were in my room made me feel loved and valued. To them, I was amazing, smart, talented—and did I mention amazing? I was these things in their minds, so I was these things in my mind. I hung the moon in their eyes and the sun rose and set over me. If you want to grow a couple of launching beliefs in the people you love, plant these words by the acre in their lives.

Each year, I would go with my parents to Disneyland. I'd take the money I had received as room rent all year and always bring something back for my grandparents. They were easy to shop for. Here's why. There was a store on Main Street that sold rock candy. These cubes of sugar were painted to look like rocks and were equal parts a pathway to obesity and a fun surprise. Each year I'd return from our trip to Disneyland and run to my grandparents' house with my big sugary surprise. Like every year before, my grandmother would say with uncontainable glee, "You bought me rocks? I'm so happy."

"No grandma," I'd say. "They're candy. Honest. Try one."

"Of course they're not. I know what a rock is, and these are rocks," my grandmother would insist.

This would go on for some time until she would finally pick one up and put it in her mouth. Then, with the amazement only matching what she had mustered the year before, she would put her hand over her mouth and say, "These *aren't* rocks. They're candy!" She had me convinced my entire young life that I was the most fun, engaging, amazing, creative, and winsome person ever to live. These became launching beliefs for me and were the birthplace of most of the joy I've found for the rest of my life.

Launching can happen when we're feeling low too. When I got sick, my grandparents would make me toast and cut it into triangles. They told me only toast cut in triangles had the ability to make me feel better. It's a half century later and when I get sick or am feeling a little low, I eat toast. You know already how it's cut—into triangles. It's the only way it makes me feel better. Launching beliefs have this kind of shelf life, and we're the ones who can build these shelves.

⌇

While the beliefs we have adopted are a part of our interior lives that can either boost momentum or get in our way, there's something external that can be equally stymieing. It's all the stuff you're already doing. It's the many things already filling your basket to the brim leaving no space for some of your new and more beautiful ambitions. There's no point in beating yourself up about this. You're not alone. We aren't born fully realizing what God made us for. We get it in installments. You have to live a little—actually, a lot—before your ambitions take shape and become fully formed in your heart. Give it some time. It's not a sprint; it's a marathon God has invited you to run with Him.

What should you do with everything that preceded this new emerging ambition of yours? Maybe you picked the wrong major or the wrong career. Maybe you're dating the wrong person or living in the wrong city. In order to get to the life you want, you need to crack the code to this question: *What do I do with the life I currently have, and what will I need to change?*

There are some beautiful things you need to hold on to even if life is a little tough right now. Your faith and family are absolutely two of them. Marriages can be hard. If you're married, you already know this. If you're not, you've already guessed it. When you take two imperfect people who want different things and put them in close proximity every day, it's bound to have some difficult moments. Hang in there. If you need some help, get it. There are plenty of good counselors out there. I've gone to a couple, and you might think about it too. There is no shame in this, only a brighter future.

It might be helpful to do a quick audit of your friend group. Certain friends might be dragging you down. Don't be too hard on them. They think they're being helpful—they're just not. You should guard your health too. The keto diet you've heard about might be more helpful than the Frito diet you've been using. Lay off the Twinkies. Find your way to the gym once or twice a year, whether you need it or not. These are the things that people who get things done, get done. Wherever you are in your life, you probably already know the ways you can change to get you closer to your ambitions. Take a step, no matter how small.

వ

If you've ever been in a really old wine cellar, you've seen racks of dusty bottles by the thousands, where wine is aging. One person has the job of giving the bottles a quarter of a twist periodically. The sediment in the wine sticks to the bottle, and if they continue to give each bottle a quarter twist, the wine stays clear. The same is true about your ambitions. Give them a quarter of a twist.

Most of us are only a quarter twist away from getting it right. It seems like a small increment, but it's probably all you need. Delta Airlines started giving airplanes only a forty-five degree pushback from the gate rather than ninety degrees. The change in angle saved a huge amount of money and hundreds of engine hours a day, which will translate into a billion dollars over time. It was just a quarter twist that did the trick.

What's your quarter-twist move? I had a young guy call me and tell me that I had made such a huge impact on him. "I've made a 360 degree change in my life," he said with a great deal of pride. I felt a little bad telling him, "Actually, that would mean you're right back where you started." I laughed. "Give it a quarter twist the other way."

I helped some friends a few years ago write a book on having multiple careers. Most people pick their careers and backfill their lives with any space left over. Give this approach a quarter of a twist too. Why not pick your life and backfill your career? Don't let your business card, your diploma, or your credentials call the shots anymore. Give your newer ambitions the permission to question some of your older decisions. I did this when I quit a perfectly good and lucrative career as a lawyer. Don't get me wrong. I loved being an attorney. I still love it. Here's what changed. I used to spend my time doing things that worked. Now I'm trying to do things that last. It is a quarter of a twist, but an important one. It's a subtle difference that will have the amount of power in your life you're willing to give it.

I grew up thinking you had one job until you retired. This is how my parents' generation lived. It's how their parents did life too. But it's a new day. It's your day. Quit playing by the old rules. I've had quite a few careers. I've had paper routes, painted houses, worked at Wienerschnitzel selling hot dogs, pumped gas, and parked cars. I'm a lawyer, a speaker. I started an airline. I'm an author, a diplomat, and many more things. This doesn't make me exceptional; it just means I'm highly engaged. You were meant to be too. Forget the flashy stuff. Be engaged with your faith, your family, and your friends. Plenty can happen when you pay a little more attention to what you're engaged in.

The reason I've had lots of careers and done many things is that I'm constantly changing. You are as well. You can have several ambitions materialize at the same time, or they can happen in a row. There's no wrong way; there's just a wrong time. Get current with yourself. Don't be who you were; be who you're becoming. Figure out how God wired you, then go do lots of that. Only strangers will remember you for your job titles. The bad jobs can get us ready for the better ones and the better ones can prepare us for the best ones. Don't lament your bad ones; just don't stay in them. Our legacy will be the amount of love and hope and engagement we release into the world, our self-awareness and our other-awareness, and our willingness to adapt and adopt new approaches as we evolve.

What we do isn't who we are. Writing a book doesn't make me an author. It doesn't even mean I'm a guy who can spell. It simply means I'm a guy who tried. I'm Sweet Maria's husband and a dad to Lindsey, Richard, and Adam (and now Jon and Ashley too). If we call ourselves speakers or writers or knife-throwers or sword-swallowers, but then some night we do a lousy job of speaking or writing or throwing knives or get the hiccups, it's not just a bad night, it's an identity crisis. Identify with your family, your friends, and Jesus. If you load up your job with your sense of purpose, you are in some dangerous territory. It's not wrong—just be careful you don't put all your eggs in a basket with a hole in it.

Who you are right now is an accumulation of all you've done and all that's happened to you. Some beliefs have limited you; perhaps you'll discover more that will launch you. You may like who you see in the mirror, or maybe you have a few bones to pick. If you're like me, it's probably a little of both. You've made some choices, and they probably didn't all turn out the way you hoped. Don't worry; that's true for all of us. We're in a constant state of becoming the next version of us—and that's a good thing. Remember that on this journey of discovering and launching your dream, you have a ton of agency over your circumstances. You can't change what happened yesterday or five minutes ago. But tomorrow is all yours, and it's up to you to decide what happens next.

Chapter 21

BE A QUITTER

The way to start something new is to quit something else.

I've spent a fair amount of time racing sailboats. I've raced in Southern California, San Francisco, and have crossed the Pacific to and from Hawaii twice. I've learned that you want a sailboat with a big sail and an even bigger keel to get the job done. The keel is the part of the sailboat that hangs down below the waterline and is filled with concrete or a heavy metal like lead. The more the wind blows, the more the keel keeps the boat steady and upright so it can move forward.

Here's what happens with keels, though. Long strands of kelp, which can be hundreds of feet in length, get stuck on them. The further you go, the more kelp you can collect. Keels are basically magnets for kelp. The deeper the keel goes, the more it catches. I once dragged a piece of kelp a long way. I had seen it trailing behind the boat as we were leaving Oahu and thought it had dropped off the keel. When we passed under the Golden Gate Bridge, there it was again. I literally had dragged it across an entire ocean without knowing it. You don't really notice right away when you have kelp on your keel. Like your life, the boat still moves. It still looks the same above the waterline. But over time, as more kelp gets caught, the boat can slow down to a crawl. The same will happen to you if you're not more watchful than I was.

You can't wish the kelp away, and you can't plan it away. The only way to get the kelp off the keel is to "back the boat down." That means you turn into the wind and let the boat come to a complete stop and let the wind push you backward. When you do this, the kelp falls off because the pressure against the keel is released. It's a practice worth adopting in our own lives. Backing down and letting a couple of things fall away will help you get where you're headed faster.

Here's how I back down the kelp in my own life. Once a year I spread everything out and ask myself, *What do I need to carry with me and what do I need to let go of?* I think about all the little decisions I make, especially the ones I make regularly, and ask whether all those decisions are working out for me. Are they serving my ambitions or getting in the way? Try it. It might be a job or a relationship or a hobby or a habit. You might decide to work out more or do it less. You might stop reading books or you might start.

Do it with your faith as well. Don't chuck your faith; slow it down, back down from some unnecessary commitments or crazy-making conversations or disagreements you've been having that are distracting you from Jesus and right the ship. I promise, you'll feel lighter and nimbler afterward. You'll be unencumbered from the drag that has been silently stealing the momentum from the most current and authentic version of you.

In addition to backing down the kelp once a year in my life, I do a smaller version of this once a week. Some of you may already know I quit one thing every Thursday. Sometimes I quit something perfectly good. I do this because life tends to always be full. We can't squeeze thirty hours of things we want to do into the twenty-four-hour bag of time we have each day. Weirdly, the thing that keeps many from moving on from things they've outgrown is coming up with a reason they can explain to others about why they quit. Start telling people you quit one thing each Thursday and you won't have to worry about putting spin on it anymore.

Try this practice for a couple of weeks. It will blow your mind. Think of it like weekly kelp removal. If something isn't working for you anymore, quit. Just do it on a Thursday so I know I'm not the only one doing it. By the way, there's nothing inherently magical about Thursday, but it is helpful in a couple of ways.

Another reason people stay stuck in something that doesn't work anymore is because they want to pick the right conditions to quit. The perfect time will never come, so stop worrying about it.

I've quit a bunch of stuff in my life. I've tried to go All-Pro on it. Here are some more examples of things I quit.

I sold my truck. It was on a Thursday, and I shared a car with Sweet Maria for a couple of years. I did it so we could spend more time together.

I quit my own law firm. You already heard this one, but it was a big thing to quit, so I'm listing it.

I quit teaching at a local university. I had been teaching at this university for more than twenty years. One Thursday, I simply quit. The reason? It was Thursday.

I quit a board position for an organization. I loved what that organization was accomplishing, but serving on a board didn't seem to maximize the time it took away from other things.

I quit making appointments. Have you noticed that what started out as a fun idea can start a long and punishing cycle of calls and emails and text messages deciding when the next conversation will happen? I found I was spending more time planning the meeting than having the meeting. I also found myself thinking about the upcoming meeting in the morning, at noon, and at 3:30 when they didn't show up at all. This all started to bug me, so on a Thursday about five years ago, I quit making appointments. It was a quarter twist on what I had been doing for a long time, and this small change has made all the difference. These days, instead of setting appointments, I tell people either to call me or simply show up if they want to see me. I let people know where I will be and they can intersect that arc or not on their terms. The people who really want to meet me do, and the others don't. I don't need to break stride while they're deciding.

So, what will you quit this Thursday? You already know what these things are. And for Pete's sake, if you are into something you shouldn't be into, don't wait until Thursday. Quit right now.

Maybe the most effective way to quit something is not to start it in the first place by learning how to say no. Clearing the path to your dream has a lot to do with learning to say no once in a while. It's difficult for many people to do this. I'm one of them. It always felt like such a buzzkill to turn down a really kind invitation. We all come by this honestly. We don't want to hurt or disappoint anyone. But we're hurting and disappointing people who want us around by always being somewhere else. They've just been too nice to tell us.

We all feel good about being invited to do one more thing. I get it. It makes us feel liked and needed, which is a good feeling. Before long, however, we're all plugged up in a scheduling nightmare. We're overextended. We've said yes to so many things that other, more important things get tossed in the back seat. The battle for our hearts is fought on the pages of our calendars. Fight the good fight, but use the right rules. You can say no. Practice it in the mirror every morning if you need to. Here are some tips on how I've learned to do this over the years.

Know when to say no. Does the dinner invitation overlap an appointment you've made to explore opportunities? Say no. Will it be life-giving to spend time over coffee or will it just be appeasing guilt or doing it out of a sense of obligation? Say no.

Learn to say no nicely. Give people your no in such an affirming way they'll be honored to get it. Say your no in a sincere and un-apologetic way. Say it with kindness and with gracious love. Don't make it a teachable moment about how great you are at saying no. Just say "no, and thank you for thinking of me."

Say no immediately. If you're like most people, you don't want to disappoint others by saying no to invitations. So we wait. Hear this: an immediate decline given in the moment is better and more honoring than a nice decline later.

Don't say "I'll pray about it." Certainly pray. Pray about everything. Pray about your next full breath, but don't cop out on an invitation by saying "Let me pray about it" if this phrase has become a placeholder while you decide without praying about it. Pro tip: Saying this doesn't make you look holy. It's just as likely to make you appear insincere.

Don't say "maybe later." Deferring is wimping out and not giving a straight answer. Don't say, "Let's meet up later," when you know the "later" never really will come. This doesn't honor people. It gives them false hope and a long-term letdown rather than an immediate honoring answer right now.

Saying yes when you want to say no can become a really harmful habit. And bad habits that deplete you can keep you from your ambitions. Before I was married, I had a really bad habit of leaving my clothes on a chair in my bedroom. Somehow the few extra steps to the closet and reaching for a hanger felt like an excessive amount of work. I'd drape shirts and jeans over the back of the chair until it started to look like it would tip over. That's when I'd switch to the seat, piling things to counterbalance everything hanging over the top. It wasn't long before I had almost all my clothes on this chair. Finding my jeans was like an archeological dig. I was as likely to find a T-Rex as a T-shirt. Eventually, once my entire closet was on this chair, I would work up the nerve to put it all back in its proper place. Then the cycle would start again, because putting stuff on the chair started feeling normal, even though it wasn't really the right place for my clothes.

Maybe this feels familiar to you, or maybe you have your own "chair" you've been piling things in your life on. It's another version of the Stockholm syndrome we've been talking about. Most of us have some aspects of our lives that are really weird, but we've been doing these things so long they feel normal—but they shouldn't. It's normal to crave routine to bring a sense of structure to our days. Ask yourself if your routine is a good one. Is it worth repeating? Does it have too strong a grip on your life, and is it keeping you from advancing on to your newer, more beautiful ambitions?

As you clear the path and offload old routines, make a sincere effort to understand why you've been doing what you've been doing. When you do this, your life may look and feel a little strange and empty at first. You will probably sense some unease and unfamiliarity. Don't back off. It's good thing. Lean into it. This is exactly the subtle shake-up dreamers like you need. You might need to put away some metaphorical clothes to clear a little headspace or clear your calendar and find some undistracted time to think. You might need to have an honest conversation with a spouse about a job switch or a shift in finances. You'll definitely need to say no to a couple of things you've been saying yes to—even good things. You'll also need to disappoint a couple of people who have come to expect a yes from you. This one can be especially tough if people have grown accustomed to your yes or you're ending your tenure volunteering for something really beautiful so you can begin something even more beautiful.

I'm kind of a quirky guy. I bet you've picked up on this. I have a little thing I do to keep all this in view for myself. I have right pockets in my jeans like you do, but I have no left pockets. I literally cut them all out. If I put my phone in my left pocket, it will come out by my shoe. It's like a bad magic trick. I do this is as a built-in daily reminder that our faith and our lives are the sum of everything we're hanging on to and everything we're willing to let go of. Try it. Get some scissors and cut out your left pockets. Guys, be careful when you do.

The reality is this: the life you're currently living is the accumulation of your choices and commitments to date. If you want a different life, an uncommon life, you'll need to change things up to make way for it. You'll need to move a couple of things from your right pocket to your left pocket. Who hurt you? Who disappointed you or let you down? What did you say yes to but need to back out of? Put all that in the other pocket. It's only eighteen inches across your midsection— okay, it's twenty inches. If you want to get after your ambitions, you'll do it. Clear the path. It might feel a little weird at first, but it will be worth it in the end.

Part 5

TAKE ACTION

Chapter 22

LIVING ON THE EDGE OF YIKES

Comfortable people don't need
Jesus, desperate people do.

When I turned sixty years old, I had three ambitions. I wanted to learn how to jump a dirt bike, hot-wire a car, and figure out how to pick a lock. I've made a little progress on each of these. I bought a KTM 500 dirt bike, and so far, I've gone thirty feet. Here's the problem—the bike only went twenty. I went right over the handlebars. I haven't quite learned how to hot-wire a car, but I broke a screwdriver and my steering column trying. Neither of these ideas turned out the way I thought they would, but I did learn how to pick a lock.

I learned by buying a transparent lock so I could see each of the seven pins inside the lock trip when I put a paperclip in and moved it around. When you're looking through the transparent lock, it's not hard to pick. It takes a little more work however, to pick the lock when you *can't* see through it. To practice this, I put my clear lock under the table as I try. Getting the lock open when you can't see it takes a lock picker's touch.

A lot of what we've done in this book has been leading up to this moment where we stop strategizing and finally take action. If you're like me, you probably wanted to skip everything before and start right here. But I've learned that you'll quickly fizzle out without a well-thought-through path toward your ambitions. My deep hope is that you have all kinds of things you can now do to get some forward movement in your life, but it's going to take a lock picker's touch to get from here to our ambitions.

There are forty waterfalls on our property in Canada, the tallest of which is hundreds of feet high. Standing in front of this waterfall will take your breath away. I've taken plenty of my friends to see it. I've even taken a few down a narrow passage that allows us to get behind the waterfall. Then we walk through the waterfall together. This is not unlike what you've been doing in this book. It's always a little mind-blowing for my friends when I invite them to step behind the waterfall and then walk through it. The water is moving fast; it has a lot of force. It's falling from hundreds of feet above them and there's a lot of it. Here's what I'm getting at. If we're going to make forward progress on our ambitions, we all need to move from *looking at* our lives and our ambitions from in front and behind and actually *step into them* at some point.

Even though my friends can't see what's on the other side when I invite them to step into the waterfall, they've got a pretty good hunch about what's there. They don't need anyone to give them more information or instructions to start. You don't either. We just need someone who will walk *through* the waterfall with us. That's what this book is about. We all need to take the step, and it will be easier if you take it with someone you trust. Just on the other side of the waterfall, many of our best ambitions have been waiting for us.

Perhaps you've got your ambitions pretty much figured out. Maybe you're still figuring out the details on a couple. Either way, it's time to walk through the waterfall. Any time I'm embarking on a new dream, I get a mixture of excitement, anticipation, and a little anxiety about what the outcome will be. There's this veil you have to step through in order to see what's on the other side. Life has a way of saying *no peeking* as we start to make steps forward. I have a little phrase that, for me, captures this moment: living on the edge of yikes.

One of my larger ambitions was to help end an armed conflict somewhere in the world. The organization I started has been at work on this mission in Uganda, Iraq, Afghanistan, and other war-torn countries. It turns out it's really hard to get people to lay down their weapons, but that doesn't mean we stop trying.

Since 1991 when its government fell apart, Somalia has been locked in a huge conflict. It has been at war with itself for almost thirty years. We've been working in a number of countries whose children grow up under the crushing weight of armed conflict. Iraq had an ISIS caliphate. Uganda had a child solider–driven insurgency. Afghanistan has been invaded by just about everyone at some point and is heavily influenced in all areas of the country by the Taliban. Somalia has a dozen clans battling each other for power, and now al-Qaeda is a huge presence.

I've stayed in three hotels in Mogadishu, Somalia. Each one has since been blown up. Somalia is a country overrun with strife and conflict. If something goes wrong in Mogadishu, you can't just write a bad Yelp review. Before you arrive, you send your blood type so they can have some on hand. You also need to give someone you trust a proof-of-life question in case you're abducted for a ransom. My answer is this: "Screw these guys. Don't give them a penny."

We've been operating in these countries in the hopes of easing some of the pain and bringing a little hope and a few more opportunities to the children. Why? It has been one of my ambitions to help young kids, and in particular, young girls, to get the shot at life they deserve, not just get shot at.

In a war, everyone takes a hit, but children, and especially young girls, always seem to pay the highest price. I want to try to level the field for them. Many people in these countries will agree that all people are created equal, but in reality boys are treated like they're a lot more equal than girls. It can be outrage or passion or both that causes us to pursue our ambitions. When you're exposed to something that connects with your passion, make it an ambition to find a way to effect some change.

Al-Qaeda's franchise in Somalia is called al-Shabaab, which means "the youth." They recruit young men to fight for them by making deceptive promises of an education. The boys learn later that they'll be educated on how to make explosive devices and take lives. Young girls don't fare any better. They aren't taught how to read and write and many are sold into forced marriages when they are barely teenagers. We didn't wait for an invitation to start schools and create safe houses in these countries. You don't need an invitation to pursue your ambitions either. You're here, you're alive, and you're able. That's all the invitation you need.

The most dangerous place in Mogadishu is inside the green zone. It's a little counterintuitive because a "green zone" sounds like it ought to be where you would expect to find the greatest protection. But the green zone is where people hide. It's where the enemy can always count on finding someone who has let their guard down. The green zone is the most dangerous place for us to be too. Yet this is where many of us live most of our lives.

If you've had ambitions for years and you haven't rolled them out into the world, it would be worth asking yourself why. Jesus never told anyone to play it safe. You were born to be brave. Act like it. Live into this truth. If you want some of your ambitions to take a leap forward, get out of the green zone in your life and take a couple of risks. If you've built some pretty high walls, you don't need to tear them all down; just build a door or two through them and get on the other side.

There is plenty of conflict and uncertainty in Somalia, but there is also boatloads of hope. Some people actively look for hope even in the midst of chaos. Be one of these people. The reason is simple. We all find what we spend the most time looking for. It's the same with our lives. Don't get wrapped around the axle despairing that your ambitions haven't been achieved yet. Delight in the fact that you have a couple of things worth doing that you haven't gotten to yet. Cultivate a spirit of hope and live in constant anticipation of what might become possible in your life if you make your way out of the green zone. There are no boxes to check, just lives to be led.

⌇

When we got off the airplane on our first trip to Mogadishu, we walked out to the SUV with tinted windows that I had arranged to meet us. In front of us was a truck with a half dozen guys on rails with machine guns. We drove out of the green zone and into the city. Mogadishu shows the wear of twenty years of civil war. Bullet holes and mortar shell pockmarks are evident on most buildings. It's like a level in Call of Duty. I have done some crazy things in my life, but driving through the narrow and often roadblocked streets behind our escort raised the hair on the back of my neck. This felt like my edge.

Mogadishu is a tricky place. It's full of beauty and hope and violence and bullets and explosions. When an attempt is going to be made on someone's life, their car will be cut off from those who are providing protection. Then bad things happen. Twenty minutes into our drive, as we were winding our way through Mogadishu, we turned down a narrow street and a car cut us off. The driver of our car turned to me and said with no small amount of terror in his voice, "This is really bad!" Now, there are two things you do not want to hear in Somalia: "This is really bad" and "I'm the captain now." I wasn't expecting what happened next. The guys with the machine guns protecting us in the truck in front started shooting. Never short on words, all I could muster in the chaos was "Yikes!"

I know it doesn't sound big, deep, and theological, but it's big, deep, and theological. Here's why. I've spent my whole life becoming more and more comfortable. I have a house, a car, a boat. Heck, I have a dog I don't even want. What I've discovered is that comfortable people don't need Jesus and don't chase their ambitions—desperate people do. If we're going to get after our ambitions, God doesn't want us living right in the middle of comfortable anymore. He wants us living on the edge of yikes.

If you want to get after your ambitions, you'll need to move away from much of the comfort you've worked so hard to create. This might mean you need a change of address to your own life. Don't worry, you'll still get important mail from your trusted friends who will support you on this adventure. Let all the rest of the junk mail get returned to the senders.

Have you noticed how comfortable people seem to have all the opinions? Desperate people just have Jesus. Look at your comfortable job, your familiar circumstances, the predictability you've spent a lifetime cultivating. Perhaps these are the things keeping you from your ambitions. Could they be holding you hostage? Living on the edge of yikes can be scary and hard, and it's sometimes even painful. That's okay. Keep breathing. Stay after it. Move toward your edge where Jesus is waiting for you. God's not leading us to the safest path forward, but to the one where we'll grow the most.

Chapter 23

10:34–10:35

The minute between planning and
taking action is the difference between
daydreamers and real dreamers.

There's a place near where I grew up called the Winchester Mystery House. Sarah Winchester moved West in the late 1800s after her husband died. He had invented the Winchester rifle and left her what would be equivalent to a half billion in cash and an additional $750,000 a month in today's dollars. This was certainly enough to keep a roof over her head. For the next thirty-eight years, she built a really weird house. It has 161 rooms, including 40 bedrooms, 2 ballrooms, 47 fireplaces and 17 chimneys, stairways that go nowhere, rooms without doors or windows, and other features that leave you shaking your head.

I have a neighbor who invited me over to see the house he'd been building for nearly eight years with no sign of being completed anytime soon. I had wondered what was taking so long and was curious to see inside. In addition to a number of odd, incomplete features, what I saw in the basement took the cake. There were tiny twinkle lights all over the ceiling. I asked about them, and get this—it was the arrangement of the cosmos on the day the owner was born. It made my birthday candles look a little meager by comparison. This place isn't quite the Winchester Mystery House, but check back in with me in a couple of years and I'll let you know if the construction is complete and he's irrigating his lawn with Perrier water. I'm not bitter.

Would it surprise you to hear that you might be doing the same bizarre things with the life you've been constructing? Here's what I mean. You build and build and prepare and prepare some more but never really move into your ambition. It's like your own Winchester Mystery House. Is everything going to fall magically into place? Of course not. It's going to take some detail work, but don't spend all your time trying to get the stars to align before you start making moves on your ambitions. Sometimes things will line up, and other times they won't. Keep making moves anyway. There's just something about *action* that makes the world want to straighten the path and flatten the road beneath your feet so it's easier to travel.

It won't always be a walk in the park. As you make some moves, you're going to face some resistance. I read somewhere that resistance to something new is like a universal constant. That rings true to me. Anyone trying to create something new, to bring an ambition into existence, will face pressures working against them. Here are a few of them.

Procrastination and lethargy. We've identified your big ambitions (and probably a lot of small and medium-sized ones too). We've captured a working list of opportunities to explore and cleared the path. With all this readiness, who would want to procrastinate or twiddle their thumbs? The truth is, a lot of people. You might be one of them. If so, take some time to figure out why.

Self-sabotage. Another dynamic I see with people who are having trouble moving toward their ambitions is self-sabotage. They don't go so far as to slash their own tires so they can't make the meeting or interview. It's usually much less obvious, but it's equally disabling. They take the nap instead of making the call. They head to the movies instead of going into the marketplace. They show up late to someone offering to help—or they don't show up at all. They might be afraid of what will happen if their ambitions start to take shape, because all the excuses will be removed. The hunt will be over. It's the moment when the dog catches the bus it's been chasing. We can't be all bravado and chasing. We need to have a plan for when things start to go right. When you blow the foam off the top, people who subconsciously sabotage their own ambitions are usually afraid of succeeding and what it will cost them in terms of security and comfort when they do.

Naysayers and haters. This might be the most common resistance you'll encounter. If you have an established group of friends or co-workers, they've come to expect certain behaviors and accomplishments from you. They see your life following a certain trajectory that doesn't make them feel threatened. Perhaps you've been in the same orbit around a peer group for years. If you remain in that place, it makes them feel like you are safe and predictable. When you change your trajectory, it can trigger a host of feelings in your friends or coworkers they may or may not yet understand as they reflect on their own dissatisfactions or lack of momentum. As you make progress, all of a sudden you can feel like you've become the enemy. It's not true, of course. You're just breaking out of the orbit you've been in. You're no longer a moon; you've become a comet.

Sometimes people get really antsy when they see others hurtling toward their dreams. Parents, friends, coworkers, even spouses . . . anyone who feels threatened by your new adventure may do things that feel like they're shutting you down. That's not their intent, and they probably don't even know they're doing it. You're picking up on the reverberations of your successes ricocheting off their own lives. They're processing what they are trying to understand out loud, using your ambition as an inflection point.

If you're married, sort it out. If you're not, practice now for the important relationships you'll have in the future. I know it will be hard, but every minute you spend on understanding your relationships is worth it. Don't try to co-opt them into your dream; help them understand where yours came from. They still might be puzzled in the end, but at least they'll understand you better. They might offer to help, or best of all, they might be inspired to do some dreaming of their own. A beautiful ambition is more contagious than the worst cold.

෴

There's a famous moment in human history where the haters and naysayers were pegging the volume needle. On December 17, 1903, after years of tinkering and experimenting, two brothers named Wilbur and Orville Wright changed history by making a successful powered flight over the sands of Kitty Hawk, North Carolina. The place was actually called Kill Devil Hills, but someone figured they wouldn't sell much merch a hundred years later with that name, so they changed it in all the books. After a coin toss, it was determined that Orville would fly the airplane they had built in their garage.

Historians say others were first to fly, but the precise moment in time when Orville pulled away from the earth was 10:35 in the morning. It was the moment we knew sustained flight was possible. Before that minute, no one knew what would happen. Nearly everyone doubted it could be done. I've always wondered to myself what Orville and Wilbur were thinking a minute before they launched at 10:34. We all wonder the same thing about our ambitions at some point. Will our ambitions fly, or will they crash and burn?

Nobody lives at 10:35. You don't, and I don't. We all live our lives and execute our ambitions at 10:34. We don't know how our lives will turn out, much less whether our ideas are going to work or not. I meet so many people in my travels, good people with great ideas, but many of them never take their ideas out of the hangar. The reason is simple. They're afraid of what they'll do if it works or afraid they'll look bad if it doesn't.

Perhaps it's validation that has you stopped a minute early. Maybe you're concerned about a big public failure, or maybe the thought of an even bigger private failure is keeping you from trying. Somehow the clock became frozen at 10:34 in your life. The good news is this: 10:35 is only a minute away from happening for each of us. That one minute is a small amount of time, but it can represent a huge shift in your life. It just requires a willingness to fail.

❧

When I first moved to San Diego for college, all I really wanted to do was surf. Honestly, I spent most of the time I should have been in class catching waves instead. Eventually, I got pretty good. During my second year in SoCal, a hurricane began churning its way across the Pacific, sending a huge swell up the coast. One of the best places to catch a south swell is a place called Sunset Cliffs. These cliffs extend for a couple of miles in each direction. To get to the water, you need to make your way down a seventy-foot cliff.

I pulled up to the beach, the dark and blackened sky ominous on the horizon. *Perfect*, I thought. *This is going to be epic.* I ran to the edge of the cliff, climbed down, and jumped into the water. The farther out I paddled, the more ferocious the waves seemed to get. I started to gather that maybe this hadn't been such a great idea.

Most of the waves were too big for me to even try to catch. Finally, one came in that was a little smaller, and I turned and paddled as hard as I could to catch it. Somehow it worked, and for a moment I was flying down the face of the wave. It didn't last long, and I went over the falls. For the next hour, I kept trying to paddle my way back out through the breaking waves without any success. In fact, each time I made it out thirty feet, the next wave would push me back one hundred feet closer to the cliffs as I drifted farther and farther away from my original entry point. Eventually, one of the waves pinned me into the cliff with tremendous force. My surfboard instantly broke into several pieces.

I kept getting pummeled and was ducking under the waves trying to get away from the cliff. Soon, I ran out of energy and had nothing left. I was sure I would die, and weirdly, I resigned myself to this truth and made my peace with God.

Unknown to me, there was a guy walking along on the top of the cliff, and he saw what was happening to me. He made his way down the cliff and got in the water with me to help me out. This is where I got saved. I don't mean "saved" the way some people in the faith community mean it, I mean "saved, saved," from my own certain death. Each year I go back to that same place on Christmas Day to give thanks to God for a guy who didn't just stand at the top of the cliff and yell Bible verses at me. Instead, he got in the water with me.

Years later, I was with two friends at Sunset Cliffs. We had ridden our motorcycles over to see a stunning sunset. It was one for the books, and after taking some photos, we headed to our motorcycles to ride back. That's when someone yelled, "Call 911!" Evidently a young man on the edge had been distracted with his cell phone, lost his balance, and fell off the cliff. We ran over to the edge and saw him on the rocks seventy feet below.

Because I'd seen how a guy made his way down that cliff years before to save me, I knew how to get down to get to this young man.

My friends and I made our way down to where he had fallen. He was in bad shape. Really bad. He needed CPR and a lot more than that. We were able to resuscitate him, but he wasn't stable. For the next hour, we tried to keep him with us and comfort him while we waited for help to arrive. When the fire trucks came and medics rappelled down the cliffs, he was dead. I felt so guilty. We did all we could, but it wasn't enough to keep him alive. One of my ambitions had been to save a life some day, and I failed when I had the chance.

But here's the thing. I'd rather fail trying than fail watching.

News of this young man's big mistake was on all the television channels. The story was about a young man foolishly distracted by his cell phone, not about the tremendous loss a family had suffered. A few months later, the mother heard I would be speaking in a city close to where she lived. Apparently she had found my name in one of the police reports. She asked if we could meet. I told her we absolutely could, and saying yes caused all the feelings of guilt and shame to flood back into me. Could I have done something different, something more to save him? I knew I couldn't blame myself for his fall, but I still felt guilty. Nonetheless, I didn't want to miss this chance to give some comfort to his mother.

That's when I remembered I'd taken a picture of the sunset. It was the same one he was looking at when he fell. I brought the photo in a simple frame and gave it to her. Instead of talking about the mistake he had made, we talked about the beauty he saw.

Our actions will not be perfect. Often, not even close. Whatever your ambition is, keep at it. Will it work? Who knows? Fail trying; don't fail watching.

A beautiful truth is that once you get your ambitions in your sights, no amount of failure will keep you from trying again—as long as you don't yield to the disappointments. If you have clarity on what you want and why you want it, you'll have what it takes to make as many attempts as needed to get there.

Do something. Descend the cliff. Paddle through the waves. Don't sit on the sidelines; get in the game. There's no way your ambition can take flight without *you* taking action. Don't think about the mistakes you might make; think about the beauty you'll see. You're only about a minute away from seeing what's next.

Chapter 24

ONE THOUSAND WORDS A DAY

Live your life undistracted.

I'm easily distracted. How about you? I'll give you some examples. Toothpicks are a distraction to me. I'm not sure why. I see them and am afraid someone will start doing some oral hygiene at the table and I'll get hit in the forehead with a stray piece of beef. Leg jigglers get me also. They look nervous, and this in turn makes me nervous. Here's another one. When I'm in a hotel room, if the phone cord is twisted into knots, I need to untangle it before I can fall asleep. Crazy, huh? I have a friend who can't stand the smell of spearmint gum. Actually, I'm not a big gum guy either. Another acquaintance can't have different vegetables touch on their plate. Still another, if someone bumps up against them on their left shoulder, they need to reach over and touch their right shoulder to even things out. I even have a friend who loses it if the toilet paper is spooling out of the bottom of the roll rather than the top. I guess we're all a little nuts, aren't we? Think about those things that distract you. You're weird too. Admit it.

When you're in the hot pursuit of your ambitions, you're going to face plenty of distractions along the way. You need to figure out how to filter all of the inputs into your life to make sure you don't get off track. That doesn't mean you shouldn't follow a whim or take a meeting if you don't know exactly what it's for. Just give yourself a heads up that you're potentially straying from the course on what you set out to do.

Here are a few ideas for you to consider to help you move forward with your ambitions without distraction.

Make a list of your ambitions. I have a foam-core board in my office that is divided into sixteen squares. Each one of these represents an ambition of mine. I'm crystal clear about what I'm focusing my attention on. I know what I want, why I want it, and what I'm going to do about it. If a new opportunity comes my way, I decide whether it's worth adding another square on the board or whether I'll pass on it. You could have three squares or thirty. The trick is to know why it made the list or didn't.

Make a date with yourself. I have a few routines I do almost every day. I'm sure you do too. Once you have an ambition in view and some moves you want to make toward it, put it in your calendar. Treat it like a date you couldn't miss and wouldn't show up for late. There's nothing wrong with telling someone, "Sorry, I can't be there because I have another commitment." Granted, it's with yourself and probably won't be the best date you've gone on, but treat it like it's the most important one you have. Setting aside and then protecting dedicated time to spend with your ambitions is a great way to make a lot of progress toward them.

Make one phone call a day. Challenge yourself to reach out to one person a day to help you make progress toward your ambition. Maybe you're trying to get through to the CEO of a company or the pope or the Dalai Lama. Don't make a list; make a call. I don't care who it is—reach out. You may not get through to the person every time or have the conversation you hoped for when you reach out. Still, taking even a small action each day can lead to huge outcomes. If you don't try, it won't happen. Give it a shot and see what opens up.

Put reminders everywhere. Whenever I'm chasing an ambition, I put reminders about it everywhere. Go beast mode on it. Write it on your hand, on your bathroom mirror, everywhere. Put sticky notes on your dashboard. Tattoo it on your dog. Hire a biplane to write it in the sky above your neighborhood or tow a banner if you need to. Send yourself a cake with your ambition written in the icing, or send the cake to me and I'll give you a call. Have your ambition engraved on a Scottish broadsword and hang it from your kilt. Make it your screen saver or ringtone—every time you pick up your phone or get a call, you'll be reminded about the future you want and the ambition that will get you there. Let your imagination run wild. Surprise yourself daily with triggers to keep your eyes on the prize. This will keep you focused and energized.

Get some administrative help. Did you know you can hire a virtual assistant for as little as one hour each week? There's a multibillion-dollar industry filled with people who want to help you. Look into it. Consider hiring your ambition an assistant. It'll only cost you fifty or a hundred bucks a month. These assistants can help you handle the details that have become impediments to you getting after your ambitions. If your ambition is to write a book, find an English major at a local university to help you—they'll never get a job anyway.

Set incremental milestones. Some ambitions are so gargantuan that they can only be accomplished a little at a time. Eventually the whole thing occurs, but it rarely happens all at once. (Actually, if you can achieve your ambition in a day, you may want to pick one that's a little bigger.) Set small milestones to remind yourself you are making progress. Have a celebration, and give yourself a reward when you get to the next waypoint. Go to Disneyland, or Coldstone, it really doesn't matter where. It matters that you're acknowledging the progress.

Get yourself a haircut or a bag of taffy when you make some headway. Whatever the task is, you can subdivide the steps toward your ambition. The more you check off the list, the closer you'll be to making it happen.

Write one thousand words a day. A lot of people who reach out to me have an ambition to write a book one day. I applaud this and think everyone has a book or two in them. The trick is to get it out of them. Books are amazing and can literally change the world. I can almost guarantee writing one will change you.

Any book I've written began with me writing one thousand bad words a day. I don't mean cuss words; I try to write bad words. This takes all the pressure off to write good ones. Later, I try to trade up these words for better ones. If I waited to write good words the first time, you wouldn't be reading this. Find the best words you have and go with those. This isn't the Olympics. You don't need to do a triple flip and plant it on the first try. Move toward your ambitions by making a series of imperfect attempts. For me, writing one thousand words a day is the difference between having an ambition that remains a concept and words that are on their way to becoming a book.

Even if writing a book isn't your ambition, consider getting your thoughts down on paper every day. If you don't write down what you're thinking about, it will be gone in twenty minutes. Remember how I told you I send myself more than a hundred emails a day? These are all thoughts I want to reflect on a little further. Later, they're the words that find their way into books, social media posts, and talks. If nothing else, writing down your thoughts will help you clarify your ideas.

∽

Doing these things will help you stay engaged and win the game against distraction. They will help you stay awake in your life as you make progress toward your ambitions. Whatever shiny thing is catching your sideways glance, move it out of sight. If you're feeling annoyed by how cold the room is, take a second to up the temperature. If your dog keeps barking at the door, give him a treat. Or do what I'm tempted to with ours: open the door and see if he'll run to the neighbor's house to find a new owner. It's normal to get distracted. Don't let that be your resting position. Endeavor to live an undistracted life, and you'll see your ambitions more clearly.

Part 6

EXPECT SETBACKS

Chapter 25

PICK THE VESPA

We don't get points for looking the part.

On one of my trips to Uganda, my son Rich came along with me to help at the school we built there. I loved having a travel buddy and wanted to do something fun together to take home a memory as a souvenir. So after compiling a list of options, we decided to go rafting on the Nile River, which flows out of Lake Victoria. Rich and I got to the outfitters, helped unload the boat and put it in the water, and we both climbed in. I was figuring out what end of the paddle to hold when the river guide pushed our small inflatable raft into the current and jumped in with us. It started out pretty calm, but it wasn't long before the river started picking up speed.

Within the first ten minutes, the guide said we were coming up on some Class 5 rapids. This was our first rafting trip, so I didn't know what "Class 5" meant. I later learned there are no Class 6 rapids, only death. When we went over the first watery cliff, I looked over at Rich. He was paddling hard and following the instructions our guide was shouting over the waves. I was too. We went through (not over, mind you) two more mountain-sized waves, then got sucked into an eddy behind a huge rock. It looked like the river might be calming down a little, and I looked over to Rich to give him a reassuring smile and a thumbs-up. But he wasn't there. He had bounced out of the boat during one of our Class 5 collisions and had been swept downriver.

Having been stuck in the eddy behind the rock for an uncomfortably long time, we paddled out and back into the rushing current to find him. We looked in the swirls of water and along the riverbank for twenty or thirty minutes without any success. I was obviously concerned and began practicing how I was going to tell Sweet Maria that I took Rich to Africa but didn't bring him back. *I thought he was with you* or *Let's make another one* didn't seem viable. Then, on the side of the river, I saw Rich holding onto a limb. We paddled hard across the current and slightly upstream. We finally made it to Rich and dragged him back into the boat. Once everyone calmed down a bit, I looked Rich square in the eyes and swore him to secrecy about the whole thing. He promised he wouldn't tell anyone, especially his mom. Want to guess the first story he told when we got home and walked through the front door with arms flailing? Humph. Kids.

Failure can be a lot like that river and those rapids. We set out after the big ambition and get swept downstream when we do something that flings us overboard. We can't fight the current; we gasp for air and look for something to cling to. When this happens, we don't need lectures or information or reproof; we just need a hand to hold that will yank us back onboard or, like Rich, sometimes all we need is a branch to hang onto until a little grace arrives.

⌢

You're going to fall out of the boat once or twice on this journey. That's okay. A setback is a failure we need to understand; an impediment is an obstacle we need to navigate around or through. These obstacles come in all forms and sizes. There are big, huge, public, debilitating setbacks, and there are small, more pedestrian ones. You have to figure out how to frame each in the overall arc of the pursuit of your ambitions. No setback is permanent if you say it's not. Sometimes you just need to alter your approach or change your game plan. Let me give you an example.

I love motorcycles, and I've had a couple. My favorite is a Harley-Davidson Softail Springer with a sidecar. I got it when a couple of us decided we were going to learn how to ride motorcycles together. For our first ride, we went across North America from Mexico to Canada. Why not go big, right?

When we started our trip, none of us had ever even taken a motorcycle out on the highway. Nevertheless, we figured out how to start them and put our back wheels over the border in Tijuana, revved our engines, and headed north. By the time we got to San Francisco, we even knew how to change gears and use the turn signals.

In all the years I've been riding, I haven't had a motorcycle license. Oops. Actually, a motorcycle with a sidecar is apparently considered a car, so I was already legal. After a couple of years, I figured it wouldn't hurt to get an add-on to my driver's license, so I headed to the Department of Motor Vehicles and signed up to take the motorcycle test. I remember getting there and thinking heaven was going to look a lot more like the DMV than some faith communities. Rich in spirit, incredibly diverse in ethnicity, and intensely on task. I just hope the line to get in doesn't take as long.

The DMV gives a written exam first and a practical exam a few weeks later. The written part asks things like whether you should go up on curbs to pass cars and do wheelies through busy intersections and shopping malls. If you guess correctly on enough of the questions, you get to take the road proficiency test. I aced the written exam, but I did daydream about doing a wheelie through the mall. For the road test, I had crossed most of North America already, so how hard could it be? I borrowed Adam's Harley chopper, put on my leather jacket, and headed to the DMV. I figured I'd slalom through some orange cones, get a burger, and head home with my license.

The examiner at the DMV smiled at me when I pulled up on the chopper wearing my leather jacket and sunglasses. I can't lie; I looked good. Kind of like the Terminator but less ripped, on fewer steroids, and with no guns. The examiner set up some orange cones and told me to weave through them without hitting any. There was also a white circle painted on the asphalt at the end of the cones. He said I had to keep my front wheel on the white circle and go around it twice. Do that and the license was all mine. Simple enough.

I started the engine and set off a couple of car alarms, grinning. The examiner didn't grin. I think one of the cars was his. I headed for the cones and, to my amazement, hit every single one of them. It must have looked like I was aiming for them. I got the front wheel on the white circle for three feet and the rest of the time struggled to stay in the same parking lot. When I pulled up to the examiner, he was shaking his head. He put a big F on my test. Always the optimist, I held the test up to him and sheepishly offered, "Fantastic?" The examiner told me I should think about pushing my motorcycle home or leaving it at the curb and taking a cab. He turned his back to me and walked away.

A month later I signed up for the test again. This time I wore a checkered windbreaker and took a yellow Vespa. I'm not kidding. It had a basket with fake flowers and the handlebars had little steamers coming out of them. I looked like a thirteen-year-old girl with a beard. As I made my way across town, children pointed at me and laughed from the back seats of their moms' minivans. I got a thumbs-up from an elderly woman crossing the street with a walker. I passed a guy at a biker bar and he blew me a kiss. I felt utterly ridiculous.

When I arrived at the DMV, I got the same examiner as before. He looked at me on my Vespa and he shook his head again. "Nice," was all he said. He walked past me with an arm full of orange cones with my tire marks still on them and told me to "try not to hit them all this time." I revved the engine on the Vespa in response. It had all the muscle of a wind-up toy.

Do you know what happened this time? I sailed right through the cones. It was like I was an Olympic slalom skier. I nailed the white circle perfectly, too, my front wheel glued to the white stripe.

After the last maneuver, I pulled up to the stunned DMV guy. I tried to pop a wheelie, but it didn't work, so I rang the bell on the handlebars as I lifted both of my feet in the air as high as they would go. He looked down at his clipboard and shot a knowing grin as he tore the top page from the perforated pad. This time, it said "PASS." He drew a smiley face on it and wrote "Looking good!" beneath it.

When there is something blocking progress on your ambition, don't bail out. Figure out what the problem is and change your approach. For my first attempt, I had two problems. First, while I looked the part of a motorcycle rider, I didn't have a lot of balance. And second, certainly Adam's Harley chopper made me look pretty awesome, but it was hard to maneuver in tight spaces. I should have been more interested in passing the test than looking the part. For me to get what I wanted, I had to change tack. I had to swap vehicles, yes, but there was more work I needed to do. I also had to shift something in myself.

People who successfully chase their ambitions are willing to lay aside some of their own pride to get there. They stop caring how they look while they're doing it. They're willing to pick the Vespa instead of the Harley.

How about you? Do you know someone who is a serial attempter but not a great finisher? They're always talking about a new hobby or a new business idea, but they never really finished the last one. Being around them can be fun, but sometimes you find yourself wondering,

Where are the outcomes for all the stuff you keep talking about? They bounce from one thing to another without sticking out their good or bad ideas and seeing them through. Don't let pride get in the way, and don't let this be you. In short, go Vespa or go home.

Getting a motorcycle license is definitely in the "small ambition" category for me, one of those quick wins that keeps you engaged with life. Don't discount the lessons you can learn from these efforts. When the big waves hit, the ones that can sweep you out from the shoreline of your dreams, you can respond with grit and grace or choose to give up. Pay attention. The small lessons are the ones that will prepare you for the big attempts. You need to decide in advance what you're going to do when you encounter a setback. The temptation to give up will be much greater than digging deep and finding out what you're really made of.

One way to steel yourself for the inevitable future setbacks you'll face is to take an inventory of how you've responded to setbacks in the past. It will give you some cheat notes on your own tendencies. If you're a person who typically rams the roadblock, where have you drawn that strength from before? If you rolled over important relationships on the way toward your ambitions, what could you have done differently? If you tend to shrink back, ask yourself where that's coming from and have some strategies in place to find your grit while you give yourself some grace. Keep these notes handy, because eventually, you're going to need them.

I also hear a lot of people in faith communities talking about doors like God is a concierge at an apartment building. "He opened the door" or "He closed the door" gets tossed around a lot. Hear me clearly: my worldview is that God orders all our steps, but we have agency over the moves we decide to make too.

Sure, I get the concept about open and closed doors. I'm just not sure I accept the premise that God is playing red light, green light with us in every situation. While I do think God cares intimately about our hearts and ambitions when they're His, I don't think He's necessarily the guy standing at the door opening and closing it. If you're a musician and sing bad songs, I wouldn't be too quick to say "God shut the door on my career." It's a hard truth, but maybe you need to get better at singing. If you're an author like me and write uninspiring words, as has happened often to me, bring it to Jesus; don't blame Him for it. What I'm saying is that it's easy to conjure up divine intervention for poor performance. Don't fall for it. Get busy getting better.

Does God engage in our lives in unseen ways? Certainly. Who knows how many guardian angels have put themselves between you and a bad outcome? If a setback comes your way, don't get off track. Hitting a couple of road bumps doesn't always mean God is trying to send you a secret, encrypted message. Maybe what you tried just didn't work out the way you hoped. What you need to really believe in your gut is that, in God's economy, nothing is ever wasted. Not your pain, nor your disappointments, not your setbacks. These are your tools. They can be used later as a recipe for your best work. Quit throwing the batter away.

God isn't like a DMV examiner tapping His pencil on a scorecard scrutinizing our every move until we get it right. He said He would be with us while we were navigating the difficulties. We all screw up—often. Keep moving ahead. We need to keep our eyes on Jesus rather than caring how we look to everyone else. If we keep it about Jesus, He promised we'd come to know more about Him while we're figuring out a few more things about ourselves.

Some things we try will work; others won't. It's that simple. Learn what you can from the successes or setbacks and move on. Don't over-identify with either. Our failures don't name us—God does. If you're not hearing the name "beloved" whispered over your shoulder when you do a major faceplant or setback, it's not Jesus doing the talking.

Chapter 26

THREE EPIC FAILS

Our failures don't define us;
they inform us.

I give myself three epic fails each year. Not just "oops" fails. I mean totally epic mess-ups. You should give yourself a couple too. Seriously, I carry around three small, red carnival tickets to remind me of the importance of realizing we're all going to mess up along the way. Having three in my wallet helps me keep track as well. If it's still the first week of January and I've used two already, I try to change the cadence a little.

A number of years ago, I used one of my tickets up in India. As you know, one of my big ambitions has been to create safe spaces for young girls in places where the deck is stacked against them. We were trying to rescue some young girls from the brothels that are so common in

India. We were ten hours South of Mumbai and had located an eleven-year-old girl trapped in a cycle of abuse and neglect.

Posing as prospective customers, we had found a dozen young girls. Videos were made and a raid was arranged. The next day, the girls were rescued and appeared before a judge who gave one of the little ones back to her parents. The problem? The parents were the ones who had sold her into the brothel in the first place. Outraged to learn she had been returned to them, we got in our car and drove through the night to find the village where the parents lived. When we arrived, a guy came at us with a knife. The reason was simple: they had just resold the little girl back to the same brothel for forty dollars.

We rushed back to the brothel to find the girl. Because the area was still white hot from the raid the previous night and the disruption of the evil business taking place there, we sent in local investigators to find her. We sat in an SUV outside the entrance to the red-light district as our people made their way to the brothel.

My cell phone rang. It was one of the investigators. "Help!" he yelled into the phone. "There's a mob and they've surrounded me!" We had our driver rush us into the district in the SUV. As we got close to the brothel, we could see a crowd of a hundred bad guys surrounding our investigator. We drove into the middle of the crowd, sprung out of the car, and tried to wrestle our investigator from the mob. The mob swelled to over three hundred bad guys. I won't lie, everyone was slugging everyone, but eventually we got our guy into the SUV.

Unknown to us, as the mob was getting violent, the driver of our car got scared and ran for his life. Inside the car and surrounded by the mob, I jumped into the front seat to start the car. Unfortunately for us, our driver had taken the car keys with him when he fled. So there we were, four of us in an SUV encircled by a mob of bad guys in the red-light district. I didn't think it could get much worse, until it did. The front window exploded as a huge rock came through, then one of the side windows shattered, then all the rest of the windows did. For the next forty-five minutes, we got stoned.

We hadn't told the police that we were going back in for the little girl. There had been no time and, frankly, police are often complicit with the brothel owners and we didn't want to risk them getting tipped off. A policeman eventually arrived to break up the crowd, and we were taken to a local hospital, then to an Indian jail. I had run through so many alternate endings for that day, and this wasn't one of them. I was feeling a long way from home that night.

Apparently one of the investigators who saw what happened called Sweet Maria. I found out later from her that through a crackling phone line all she could hear was, "Bob and his friends were stoned by a mob . . . he's in . . . the hospital . . . he's been taken . . . to a jail," then his cell phone clicked off. Maria collapsed on the floor. It had been an epic failure at every level.

Here's what I'm getting at: the bigger and more audacious your ambition is, the more epic the failure can be. Yours might be across the ocean or across the street, but the possibility of an epic failure is always there.

When you fail epically, you're not alone. The Bible gives you lots of people to relate to. Take Abraham for instance. You can read in Genesis how he continually went his own way without consulting with God first. Yet God told Abraham that the entire worldwide family of faith would be traced directly through him. David had some pretty epic fails everyone heard about, including adultery and murder. Yet the genealogy of Jesus came through him. He's even described as a man after God's own heart. How crazy is that? As a culture, we have sent presidents packing and excommunicated pastors for much less. Moses killed a guy, for Pete's sake, yet God picked him to deliver His words on a stone tablet about how we should live. He then led a nation of people to a promised land. God shows us, over and over again, that our failures don't disqualify us; they prepare us.

Truthfully, most people are more concerned about others *seeing* them fail than they are about *actually* failing. So we all, to some degree, try to act like we're not failing at all—ever. I have yet to see a social media post showing someone bailing out on a relationship or giving in to a temptation. I haven't seen one picture of a guy giving up fifty feet from the summit or cheating on a test or losing his temper or getting audited by the IRS or yelling at his kid. Our need for validation can mess with our heads. We wonder, are we the only one having big and small failures pockmark our days? Don't be tricked into thinking you're the only one having to trudge through difficulties. Failure creates an invitation that faking will always miss. Tear up a ticket or two. It's okay. On the other side of an epic fail can be equally epic beauty and authenticity, which can only be born out of understanding our desperate need for love, grace, and help.

When you face your setbacks, a flood of lies will come at you—and fast. *You're not good enough. You don't have what it takes to do this. What were you even thinking trying to accomplish this? You'll never get this done. Don't waste your time.* When you experience a failure on the path to your ambition, remember this: just because you messed up doesn't mean you are disqualified. Instead it gives you the street cred you need before people will really listen to what you have to say.

Failures can also lead to new, important discoveries. I've already mentioned that it took almost a quarter century to build the Lodge in Canada, including five years to rebuild after it burned down. This was a plot twist we weren't planning for, but it revealed a hidden narrative in the story. Let me explain.

I'll never forget when we got the call that it was up in flames. It was the middle of the night when my phone rang. When we're not at the property, it gets looked after by some wonderful people who have helped us for decades. They saw the glowing red from where they were and smelled the smoke. By the time they realized the Lodge was on fire, it was totally consumed in flames, and they knew it would be a total loss.

In the aftermath of the devastation, we pieced together what caused the fire. The Lodge was made entirely of wooden logs, which needed to be restained periodically. Evidently, stain is highly combustible, and the application is like dousing your whole house with lighter fluid until it dries. It also turns out the painters left a heap of oily rags in a pile. The stain residue superheated and spontaneously combusted.

Sweet Maria and I left the next day to inspect the damage. We knew going up that it really meant saying goodbye to a lifetime of memories.

The loss of the Lodge made me really sad, but it derailed Sweet Maria. She gave me permission to share this with you. We went to a counselor together, and the counselor asked her, "What was the hardest part about losing the Lodge?" And she said, "It was the only place on earth that I felt safe." As the counselor kept asking questions, it turns out we weren't talking about the Lodge anymore. We were talking about a guy who decades ago did something horrific to her. I told Maria, "If it took our Lodge burning down for you to get real with this, to get authentic with this, I would have lit the match myself."

Losing the Lodge was a huge setback for my family. But without that deep pain, Sweet Maria wouldn't have recognized this other unhealed wound. Know this: God will burn down whatever it takes to get to the truth of our lives.

You are going to face setbacks on this adventure. Some of them will be small. Others may knock you flat on your butt for quite a while. The fault for the setback may lie with someone you trusted who let you down. You might even be the cause of your own setbacks. If you want to take a big step toward your ambitions, decide right now you'll give grace to yourself while you're waiting to give forgiveness to others or receive it from them.

Have a game plan for how you'll respond. Carry a few red tickets with you. Write yourself a letter labeled *Open in case of a setback*. Cultivate things in your life that are taller and truer than the failure you're standing next to. Don't sulk or get sucked into an eddy of self-pity when something goes wrong. Keep your head up. Don't shade it; admit it. You messed up. Doing this doesn't mean you are a mess-up, it means you're a dreamer who's willing to take some risks, get a few scrapes, clear away the ashes, and build some new foundations.

Part 7

SUSTAIN BELIEF AND LAND THE PLANE

Chapter 27

CHECK YOUR ROPES

Anchor yourself to the right things.

The first time I was introduced to rock climbing, I was in college. I lived with a friend of mine named Jack and three other guys in a one-bedroom apartment. It was kind of like couch surfing, except nobody ever left, so it was just a lot of guys living on couches. Our apartment was a pitiful place, and we each paid only forty-eight dollars a month, which included parking and utilities. It was that bad. Jack and I found the place. Then we found a couple of roommates from an ad we put in the local newspaper. For the price and living arrangement, we weren't surprised when it turned out they were both a little odd. Shortly after moving in, one of the guys started rebuilding his car engine in the living room. If we couldn't find a spoon in the morning for cereal, we'd grab a socket wrench and throw it in the dishwasher afterward.

Our other roommate was a big-time rock climber, and I asked him if he'd teach us. He taught us how to do what he was good at, like how to climb, and we showed him the stuff that came naturally to us, like how to fall. He also showed us how to belay each other. This is what it's called when one person is climbing and the other person takes up the slack on the rope so if the climber slips, they don't fall very far. Sometimes you belay from below, and other times, when you get to the top and someone is climbing up toward you, you belay them from above. Either way, our roommate told us that when we're belaying someone, they're depending on us to carry their weight. Everything about belaying safely is tied for first place in importance, but he told us one of the most critical steps is to anchor yourself into the rock first so if the climber falls, they don't pull you over with them.

With one lesson under our belts, Jack and I confidently headed out to the cliffs alone the next weekend. We flipped a coin to see who would lead up the rock face and who would follow. The person who lost went first, and that person was (predictably) me.

Jack tied in and I started climbing while he belayed from below. The person who is leading attaches the rope to carabiners so if they lose their footing they won't fall far, as the person below holds them in place with the rope. It happened to me more than once that I'd lose my grip and find myself dangling from the rope after I'd popped off the rock face. Because Jack was anchored in, he could hold my weight, and he looked up patiently knowing soon I would get my hands and feet on something secure and keep climbing.

It took a while, but I made it to the top of the cliff and did a couple of fist pumps. I hurried to get the rope ready to belay Jack from above. I sat down, told Jack he was on belay, gave the rope a couple of tugs to let Jack know I was ready, and he started climbing. When Jack was about halfway up the cliff face, I looked down at the tangle of ropes at my feet and realized that in my enthusiasm about having made it to the top, I had completely forgotten to tie myself into the rock. Sure, it looked like I was tied in, but I actually wasn't. Instead of tying myself to a rock that wasn't going to move, I had mistakenly clipped myself right back into the rope, which wasn't tied into anything.

As you chase your ambitions, there will be some days or even entire seasons when you're not moving as quickly as you want. We've already discussed that you're going to face some setbacks. I've had a couple, and you will too. When the shine wears off the penny in your process, don't try to fake it with the people around you. Don't settle for merely looking like you're tied in to your faith and to things that last. It will not help you to have people think you're anchored in when you're actually not.

Don't mistake the tangle of activities, like so many ropes around your feet, for a purposeful life. There's a big difference between looking prepared and being prepared. If you find you've lost the plot, take the break you need to tie back into your faith and understand your beliefs. Let the people around you know you want them to find a safe place while you do it.

The Bible talks a lot about rocks. In fact, God is often described as a rock—someone immoveable who we can always depend on. The people I've known who have tied their lives into Jesus didn't do it because they thought He'd keep them from falling; instead, they did it because they believed He could handle the weight of their failures when they did.

If you want to get after your ambitions, you need to be tied to a rock rather than all the things around the rock, like I was. We'll need it if we're going to bear up under the weight of our setbacks yet continue to sustain belief. This is going to take equal parts grit and resolve, but you've got plenty of both if you're willing to access them.

After I realized I wasn't tied in, I called down to Jack as calmly as I could, and I told him to find a ledge where he would be secure while I tied myself back into the rock in several places. The point here is to be honest with the people around you. Tell them you need to take a break and tie back in. There's no shame in this, only wisdom.

Once I got myself sorted out, I told Jack he could continue up the face, and he eventually made it to the top. The funny thing is, Jack never knew he was in trouble. I didn't know I was in trouble, either, until I paused long enough to assess my situation. It may seem counterintuitive, but sustaining belief looks like situational awareness of your circumstances, acknowledging the predicament, tying back in, and getting back to the work at hand. Be picky and wise about what you tie yourself to. It's one of the most important decisions you'll make in this process.

When I realized Jack was in trouble because I had made a mistake, I also needed to be picky about what I said and how I said it. I was calm and truthful, not panicky and blabbering. The words I spoke to Jack to get him back to safety were incredibly important. I probably wouldn't have more than one chance to get it right. Since then, I've tried to think about all my words with that same kind of intention, though I don't always do a good job. This lesson was reinforced with even greater depth when I got a call from a woman who read my first book.

A friend gave it to her after she received some really bad news. She had just learned she had a brain tumor. I was so sad for her and couldn't imagine how frightening receiving that news would be. She told me the news had been washing over her in waves. Sometimes she felt like she was swimming and, at other times, drowning.

She also told me something surprising. Having the tumor wasn't the scariest news she had learned. The doctors had told her they would need to operate on her the next week to remove it. That wasn't the scariest part to her either. In order to get to the tumor, they had to go through the part of her brain that lets her speak. She called me to have one of the last few conversations she would likely have. I was the one without any words.

I've never counted how many words I say each day. It must be thousands. I read somewhere we use between ten and twenty thousand words per day. I'm not sure if that's right or wrong, high or low, but I know we all use a lot of them.

I asked my new friend what she was saying to her friends in these last few days before the operation. I mused that if I only had a few days left to speak—*ever*—I'd probably break all the words-per-day records. It'd be a hundred thousand words, bare minimum. You know what she told me? "Honey, I'm being really picky about what I say."

I was perplexed. "Picky? You mean you're not saying many words?" I replied.

"Yep. I want the few words I have left to mean more than all the words I've ever said before."

She wanted to say beautiful, true things—not just more things.

I asked my new friend if we could reconnect the Friday following the operation. She graciously accepted. I wanted her to know that there would be people available to her even though she was losing this one important part of her humanity. When the time came to get in touch with her, I dialed the number. After it rang a couple times, we were on the line together—and neither one of us said anything. Our silence had become more powerful than a boatload of words.

If you need to sustain belief in your ambitions, don't default to hand-wringing, idle conversations laced with despair and disappointment. Be picky about your words. You only need a few of them. Pick better ones, more meaningful and lasting ones. Here's three to start with: "Be not afraid." You'll know if these are the words for you. If there are different words that give you clarity, use those.

I have a friend, and he and his wife lost their beautiful child. No one saw it coming. A woman heard about his loss and said, "I know exactly how you feel . . . my dog died too." I can imagine what went through his mind in that moment. He took a long breath and rather than responding with legitimate outrage at equating one thing with the other, he put his hand on her shoulder and asked, "What was your dog's name?" He realized that pain is pain, loss is loss. God doesn't grade these things on a curve.

You're going to encounter some difficult people along the way. Guess what? You're one of them. When you do come across someone who is a little much to handle, be picky about the words you speak. We're not umpires calling balls and strikes on each other. When we're operating at our best, we're more like base coaches cheering people on as they run as fast as they can toward home. Jesus modeled this. He didn't vet the guy on the cross next to Him. He didn't ask "What were you in for?" or "Do you feel bad about what you did?" Instead, He turned to him and basically said, "I'll see you in paradise." If someone is a pill to you, don't worry about it. You don't need to swing at every pitch. Tell them you'll see them in paradise and walk away. The only time I'll raise my voice is when I'm yodeling—and I've never yodeled.

Your words have tremendous power. They might be the most powerful thing any of us really have. Use them wisely. Use them sparingly. Unlock their power with intention. Recognize that a few right words have the power to sustain you.

Your words matter as much as your actions. Pick good ones. The stupid shelf is really wide and always has plenty of things on it to grab. Don't go there. Reach a little higher. When people have done this for me, they've become unforgettable.

Chapter 28

GROUND EFFECT

Get your wheels on the ground.

I was in India meeting with people who had been sold into slavery in a system known as "bonded labor." We met at midnight in a small church. This church wasn't the kind of place you would think of when I say *church*. It was a humble one-room building where the pastor would meet with people from the village. There was no electricity, only candles. No pews, only a few pieces of furniture and a small wooden table with one of the legs missing. In that makeshift church, they would share more than what they were learning about Jesus; they shared all they had, even though it was meager by most standards.

On top of the table were two clay jars of rice. As the bonded laborers came inside from the darkness, I asked the pastor what the jars were for.

He told me that one jar was for everyone to give what they could; the other was for taking what they needed. There was only one rule. They could give or take as often as they wanted or needed, but it could only be one handful at a time. The pastor told me that one handful was enough to make a meal; one handful was enough to give a meal. What was most amazing is that neither jar was ever empty. Isn't that beautiful?

Around the same time as this trip, I was discovering an ambition to put on a conference. I had spoken at a lot of them but never hosted one. Not only did I think it would be fun, but this pastor inspired me to see if we could build a new economy at the gathering. Let me explain.

To have a conference you need to have a venue, so a couple of friends and I decided to rent out the convention center in a city that doesn't host many of these types of conferences because honestly, it's not that nice. It turns out that renting this place was really expensive, and they made me put up our house as collateral. I called some friends who play music and speak all around the world. We offered them pizza and bus fare home if they'd come. Within a couple of weeks, the conference sold out.

As we put together our program, I couldn't stop thinking about what I'd learned from my pastor friend in India and how the people in his village took or gave a handful of rice to meet each other's needs. We decided to do the same thing at the conference. We had two huge bowls by the lobby doors. We put a pile of money in one bowl and let people know they could take what they needed. The other bowl was empty. I explained one bowl was for taking and the other was for giving. They could take what they need or, if they wanted, give what they had. We didn't police the bowls or watch what was happening during the conference. Our job isn't to see if people are being fair and equitable; we set the table and let people decide what business to do when they get there. At the end of the first evening, we left the bowls out for the convention center workers to take what they needed too.

When we ended the event, the "giving bowl" was brimming over, and the "taking bowl" had plenty left too. We gave everything in both away. I don't know how much money flowed through those bowls, but I'm pretty certain it was a lot. We made our own economy around that pastor's idea. You can too. Find a community of people who want to lean into one another and share everything they have. Be one of those people. This will be the path toward landing your ambitions.

A story from this experience eventually made its way back to us. One woman at the conference took home a five-dollar bill. A year later, I was speaking at another event when this same woman came up to me. She handed me a duffle bag the size of a carry-on. It was bulky and heavy. I unzipped it, and it was stuffed to the top with five-dollar bundles rolled together with rubber bands. It must have looked like a drug deal going down.

It turns out this woman had an ambition when she came to our conference. She wanted to help hurting kids in Africa. She didn't want to go across an ocean, so she did it at the local craft store. She told me she used the money she had taken from the bowl and bought five dollars' worth of beads. Sure, it was only a handful of beads, but it was enough to make something. She sold her jewelry and bought ten dollars' worth of beads with the proceeds. You see where this is headed. She kept increasing her bead count, and eventually accomplished her big ambition. She did all of this one handful at a time.

She didn't just circle the airfield, she landed the plane with her idea. You can too. Are you ready?

∽

You probably have some trustworthy answers to life's three big questions: *Who are you? Where are you? What do you want?* You're in the right seat now. What are you going to do about what you've discovered?

Hopefully you've gotten more engaged with the world around you and the possibilities within you. You've identified some people to travel with on this journey and have done a personal inventory of the capabilities you have and the fears that have held you back.

You've given specific expressions to your ambitions, created a punch list of actions to take, made a couple of leaps to give you momentum, and cleared some space in your life to make way for new attempts. You've probably even done a few things to get started. If you've had a couple of setbacks, that's good. It's like you've put down the landing flaps.

If you want to turn your five dollars of ambition into a large bowl of completion, it's time for you to land the plane.

෴

If you've flown in an airplane, or next time you're in one, take notice of what happens right before you touch down. The pilot decelerates the plane—sometimes they even cut the engines after they get over the numbers at the end of the runway. When they do this, the plane is still hovering around ten or fifteen feet above the ground. Have you ever wondered why the plane seems to float there over the runway for a while before touching down? It's a phenomenon called "ground effect." The wind traveling past the underside of the wing pushes against the ground and then pushes up against the wing from below. When you're pursuing your ambitions, you can experience some ground effect too. It can keep you ten feet over your ambitions.

There's something safe and comforting about the planning process, isn't there? This happens to our ambitions all the time. The last step in this process is to stop all the planning already. Book the flight. Buy the ring. Host the first meeting in your living room. Whatever it is, stop hovering ten feet above your dream. You're going to need to pitch forward a little bit more and get your wheels on the ground.

As you do this, don't aim for perfection; look for proof that your ambition is taking shape in the world. Don't think it will all go smoothly. Be ready for the jolt when you touch down. Block out all the reasons this could go wrong or why you shouldn't try. Circle back to all of the insights and clarity you've gathered through this book as your reminder that *your ambition is worth it. All of it.* It is worth everything you can throw at it. It's worth every sacrifice you'll make to turn your idea to reality.

It may seem ironic or counterintuitive, but the ultimate goal of this book is for you to put it down and get going. Of course, come back and reference it as needed. If you only think about what you read or doodle in the margins, that's all you have—a bunch of squiggles. Somewhere out there, someone is praying that you'll put down your pen and spring into action. Stop talking about what you want to do some day. Get started. Don't wait for the right day, a full moon, or a fairy to land on your nose. Make up an eighth day of the week if you need to. Call it "Startday."

⌔

One of the last things they taught me when I was training to get my pilot's license is how to respond when the engine stops midflight. That got my attention. Here's what they had me do: we flew a few thousand feet up in the air then practiced cutting the power to the engine. Before we did, I looked at the instructor in the copilot seat and asked, "You're sure you want me to do this, right?" Believe me, it's more than a little unsettling to pull back all of the power from the engine. If you're like me, the whir of airplane engines can be a little annoying, but far worse is complete silence. In that moment, you realize a really good airplane just turned into a really bad glider.

What a pilot does next has a lot of parallels to how you'll land your ambitions.

When the engine fails, they teach you this process: "Pitch, pick, and point." Pitching means you push the controls to the plane forward and "pitch" it toward the ground. Doing this takes carving that new groove in your brain we've been talking about because when the propeller stops spinning, the earth doesn't feel like your friend anymore. If you go with your instincts and pull back on the flight controls, something worse will happen: you'll stall out and crash for sure. We've all stalled out with our ideas. It's easy to pull back when it happens. What I'm learning is to pitch forward.

The second thing you do makes a little more sense than the first. You "pick" where you're going to land. It can be a field or a road or a parking lot. The idea is to pick something, anything other than a body of water or herd of cattle. If you don't pick anywhere, you'll lose the opportunity to influence the outcome. The same is true in our lives. I've felt the most disoriented when I haven't picked where I wanted to land next with my ambitions. Being a good picker is worth the effort, because your landing spot will impact you and whoever is with you on the adventure.

The last thing to do after pitching forward and picking your landing spot is it to keep "pointing" at what you picked. It sounds simple enough, but in flying and in life, it's easy to get distracted. We're all prone to wander. Our eyes wander, so do our interests and attention. When any of these happen, we stop pointing at the right things. Rather than pointing at beautiful, truthful things, we sometimes point toward dark ones or ones that are merely entertaining. Paul talked about fixing our eyes on Jesus. Certainly do this and as you do, notice all the beautiful ambitions of yours that are adjacent to Him. If we don't, instead of pointing at things that will be lasting and purposeful, we settle for things that merely work or are easily available. I may land in a cornfield, but what I've learned from flying is that instead of picking everything and aiming at nothing, I need to pick something worth pointing all my energies at. Once I do, I don't take my eyes off of it, and I keep pointing at it in the best or worst of circumstances. Do these things and you'll land your plane as you launch your ideas.

Chapter 29

MATTERS OF THE HEART

Sometimes the biggest ambition
starts with the smallest whisper.

I have a friend named Kelly. She and her husband, Craig, live not far from me in Southern California. I met these two kind souls more than a couple decades ago, and we've been friends ever since. They have a joyful sense of adventure and anticipation about them, and it's magnetic. They'll pull you in like you were made of metal. As our friendship grew, I asked them about how they had met each other, what their ambitions were, and what things they had overcome together. I had no idea what I'd learn about them.

Craig and Kelly both love the outdoors. They take twenty-mile hikes up steep mountain trails to relax; then when they get back, they go for long runs just to get some real exercise in. One day Kelly came home from a hike and was feeling a little lightheaded. Instead of her heart beating slow and strong as it always had, it was beating rapidly, and it wouldn't slow down even after she rested for a while. She went to a doctor to have her symptoms checked out, and they told her it was all in her head and she was probably just having a panic attack. If you've never had a panic attack, it's like having a gunnysack put over your head so you can't breathe and at the same time having a lightning rod stabbed into your heart. I'm told it feels in equal parts like you just might die and you just might live.

These kinds of things aren't scary to a girl who walks on razor-edge cliffs wearing a sixty-pound backpack for fun. Still, the panic attack explanation didn't sound right to her. She took the doctor's advice and met with a psychologist a couple of times, who gave her some useful input. Down deep, though, Kelly sensed there was something more to it.

A few weeks later, Kelly's heart started racing again. This time it was galloping even faster than before. When your heart abandons its regular rhythm and beats this quickly, the muscles just slap at the blood instead of opening and closing to move it through the body. The consequence of this is that the oxygen the body needs isn't getting to where it's supposed to go. Kelly made it to a hospital, her head still spinning. Something was definitely wrong. The doctor in charge figured out that this was not a head thing as the other doctor had suspected. It was a serious heart condition. Kelly's heart had been invaded by a virus and was about to stop beating. No one really knows where she picked it up. She was transferred to UCLA Medical Center where she promised herself and the people she loved that she would live. This was the ambition she was pointing at. Kelly is a fighter. She's as scrappy as she is kind, and this was going to take everything she had.

The doctor came into Kelly's room a short time after she arrived and had been hooked to a dozen machines monitoring her failing heart. He pulled up a chair next to Kelly, flipped through some charts, and gave Kelly the chilling news that her heart was irreversibly damaged and was dying. Her options were grave. She would either get a new heart or she wouldn't survive.

～

Alice lived on the East Coast, loved horses, and was quick to say yes to any chance to ride. She had ambitions like all of us. She wanted to make her life count for something bigger than herself. She wanted to be part of something that would outlast her, as we all do. She had a daughter she loved, and they would blow bubbles together and whisper to each other about the adventures they would have together.

It was a beautiful fall day and Alice was riding. In a tragic moment, she was involved in a terrible accident. It wasn't the injury that ended her life but a brain aneurism that arose out of a complication while she was at the hospital. She was pronounced brain-dead. It was a moment of unspeakable grief for the family. But Alice had been ready for something like this and her donor card allowed doctors to use her organs. The paperwork was organized, and although Alice's life was over, she still had one more gift to give away.

The phone rang at Kelly's hospital. The administrator told her and Craig the words they prayed to hear. "We've got a heart for your wife."

～

The skilled doctors and nurses successfully replaced Kelly's heart with Alice's. When the operation was completed, the doctor gave Kelly's new heart a flick and it started to beat in her chest. What would have been a death sentence even years before was changed because of a beautiful collision of overlapping ambitions: a team of doctors who had pursued their ambitions through decades of training and needed to learn how to transplant a heart, a woman named Alice who wanted to make a difference in the world by being part of something that would outlast her, and Kelly's ambition and determination to climb more mountains.

Heart replacement is a massive and complicated surgery, and it has ongoing physical effects on Kelly. By necessity, the operation requires severing many of the nerves that connect the patient's head and heart. As a result, the correct messages aren't always communicated from one to the other. It's complicated, but by default, Kelly's new heart always thinks it is at sea level. This poses complications for a woman who loves to climb tall mountains. Instead of giving up that passion, she had to learn how to coax her new heart into understanding its surroundings.

She literally has to whisper to her heart now. When she starts a climb, she needs to let her new heart know what she's doing is really hard work and it's got to beat much harder. Speaking this kind of truth is what makes the climb possible. Similarly, she has to whisper to her heart again after she gets to the summit so that her heart knows the work is done and it's time to rest.

⌒

The healing for Kelly following the surgery was not just physical, but also emotional. While endlessly grateful for the gift of life, Kelly had never truly come to peace with someone else's heart in her chest and the loss it represented for the other family involved. It was confusing and hard to live in a constant state of gratitude and grief. She couldn't shake it. Still, she knew she had received a second chance at life and was not going to waste it.

Kelly and Craig continued to climb mountains. They used Kelly's setback as an opportunity to grow the ambitions they still had and to motivate others. Drawing attention to the beauty and power of organ donation, Kelly has been climbing the world's highest peaks with a brand-new heart. She's climbed Half Dome in Yosemite National Park, Mount Whitney, Mount Kilimanjaro—one of the world's seven summits—the Matterhorn, New Zealand's Mount Rolling Pin, Argentina's Cajón de Arenales, and many others. She hasn't wasted a second of the new life she was given.

One day the phone rang at Craig and Kelly's home. No one was there to answer. Craig had been away from the house and Kelly was visiting her parents. When Craig came home, there was a message on their telephone answering machine. It was a young voice. "Is this Kelly's phone number?" After a long pause, "I lost my mother a while ago, and I read about Kelly in an article." There was another long pause, then she said in a small and uncertain voice packed with emotion, "I think you have my mom's heart." The message ended.

Craig was stunned and unsure about what to do next. Was this legit? Should he call her back? If it was Alice's daughter, should they try to create a relationship with her? He knew that Kelly wrestled with the loss that gave her a second chance. Maybe this was a chance for healing; maybe it would make things worse. Still, the thought of ignoring this young woman was unthinkable to Craig. He called her back, and they connected all of the information together. She was right. It was Alice's heart beating in Kelly's chest. But Craig was still unsure how it would affect Kelly.

Craig and Alice's daughter spoke several times about her mother, her ambitions, the gift she gave to the world, and the gift of life she gave to Kelly. Craig hesitantly shared that Kelly, while ever grateful for Alice's gift, was burdened by the loss it represented. Alice's daughter, it turned out, was just as kind as her mother. She had an idea—one that could bring healing to Kelly and closure for her and her mom. They decided it would happen on their next climb.

~

Kelly and Craig had flown to Japan in their work to raise awareness around organ donation. They were there to thank the government for passing a new law, making organ donation possible for many more people. They also wanted to bring attention to the new legislation by summiting Mount Fuji. They both had their packs as usual, but Craig's had a couple of special items in it.

They had been hiking all night, and dawn was slowly breaking as they reached the summit. The sun rose as they looked down at a sea of clouds from the mountaintop. It was a stunning sight. As they set down their packs, Kelly and Craig looked out over the expansive terrain below them with a familiar swirl of gratitude and grief washing over Kelly. As they had done on other climbs, they brought bubbles to blow from the summit and watched as they drifted into the crisp morning air.

After they had a snack and drank some water, Craig walked over to Kelly, holding a small container in his hand. Kelly looked at him, confused.

"What's this?"

"There's been something I've been wanting to tell you," Craig said, "but I had to wait for the right time." After a pause, he continued. "Alice's daughter reached out to us while you were visiting your parents. She left us a message on the answering machine, and I've spoken with her a few times."

Kelly looked at Craig, stunned and speechless.

"I told her how you were struggling with the grief of their loss. She wanted closure too. She thought it would be meaningful for you both if you'd be willing to scatter her mom's ashes on this mountaintop."

Kelly started to cry. The weight she had carried was constant, and sometimes she even kept it to herself. She didn't know if she'd ever move past it. But now, through the thoughtfulness of the daughter, she thought it could be possible. She held out both hands to take what had been brought for her.

They both walked to an outermost part of the summit. The sun was at full blaze now, casting light on the ripples of clouds below. A slight wind blew the crisp air. Kelly set down the nondescript jar, her eyes closed.

"I'm so sorry for what happened to you, and I'm so grateful for the chance you've given me. I promise to live my life in a way that honors yours." She opened the jar and tilted it as the wind swept across a sea of light.

Then she whispered to her heart, "It's time to rest."

EPILOGUE

So much of Kelly's story contains what we've been talking about throughout this book. Perhaps you need to do the same with your heart. Are you going through a difficult time with your work, your relationships, your ambitions? If you are, get real and talk to your heart about it. Let your heart know it's not just hard, it's a *really* hard circumstance you're in. Maybe you need to whisper to your heart that it's got to beat harder and stronger than ever before. Find a couple safe people to share your feelings with. Find a counselor; there are plenty of good ones out there. This is the kind of emotional wisdom it's going to take to climb your mountain.

Are you at the other end of the spectrum? Have you been going Mach 5 with your hair on fire for years? Perhaps your life has been in constant defibrillation. Sure, you're making lots of moves and maybe a pile of cash, but you're not getting anywhere. Maybe you need to whisper to your heart that it's time to rest.

Just like Kelly whispers to her heart, it's time you whispered to yours too. There may be a lot of things you need to say, but let's start with this: *It's time for me to dream big.*

THE DREAM BIG
FRAMEWORK

Reflection Questions and Action Ideas

Welcome! This is the section I mentioned at the beginning of the book where I've gathered some questions and actions that you can use to discover your most worthwhile ambition and make some moves toward it. Think of this section as your dream hub. You can use it as you go through each chapter or wait until you're done with the book. It's completely up to you. I think it will help you gain the clarity, confidence, and momentum you need to turn your ambitions into realities.

A lot of what you'll find here are the same kinds of prompts and exercises I use with groups in my live Dream Big workshops. Thousands of people just like you have wrestled with these very things and have made great progress. I know you will too.

I recommend that you have a dedicated space where you can

capture all your thoughts. You'll be making lists, writing letters to yourself, answering some hard questions, and jotting down steps you can take to move toward your dream. Think about getting a journal or a legal pad or a Google doc—whatever works best for you. Just be sure to capture your thoughts and responses. These answers, in a way, are *you*. This is the good and hard work of understanding who you are and how God made you so you can unearth the ambitions that may have been sitting dormant in your heart. We're going to move them from staying inside of you to impacting the world around you. Are you ready?

Part 1: Getting Ready to Dream Big

Chapter 3: Get Under the Ice Cap

We talked about "getting under the ice cap." Down there is where you start your journey toward the three big questions: *Who are you? Where are you? What do you want?* Here are some questions you can think about to start the process of discovery.

Chapter 4: Who Are You?
- Are there some recurring themes in your behavior and choices? For instance, do you tend to act out of fear or a sense there will never be enough?
- Do you think *you* will never be enough?
- Do you live life out of a fake bravado or think you have to always please others?
- Take some time to explore *why* you do what you do. It's okay if this takes more than a few minutes, especially if you're asking yourself these questions for the first time. Take as much time as you need to express what is real, honest, and true about you.

Chapter 5: Where Are You?

- Remember, think *biography*, not *geography*. Are you confused about which major to choose? Do you feel stuck in your career choice but don't know how to change it? Are you up to your eyeballs in debt? Are you happy in your marriage or other important relationships?

- Obviously, there are a million and one questions we could ask. But I bet you already have a sense of where you are right now in your life. Take some time to describe exactly where you are *right now*. Be brutally honest. It's okay if you're not completely jazzed by your answer. Just about everyone wants something to change in their lives, including me.

- Think of a close friend who you can get honest with, then complete this statement: "I'm meeting X at Starbucks to tell them exactly where I am right now." Then send the text or make the call to set up the time.

Chapter 6: What Do You Want?

- So much of this book is about finding the right answers to this very question. In this part of the framework, we're going to make a first attempt at creating a list of what you want. Do you want a bigger house? Do you want to make working the soup line a Christmas tradition? Do you want to hike the Pacific Crest Trail or finally get to Paris? Do you want to lose weight or reconcile with your dad? It can be all this and more.

  Your list will be totally unique to you, and it will probably get you pretty excited. That's the point! Don't worry about "editing" the list to make it look more noble or holy. Just be honest. Think about every single thing you're dreaming about right now and get it on a list. Go buy a legal pad with at least fifty blank pages. It's okay if you fill one of them or all of them. Just make sure to capture *everything*. Later on we'll work toward curating the list and arranging your dreams so they make a constellation of possibilities you can actually work toward. For now, just write it all down. Have fun!

- What if "future you" could write a letter to "current you" about all you've accomplished and experienced on this journey? What would that future you say to help and encourage the current you? Take fifteen to twenty minutes to write that letter. Stuff it in an envelope, address it to yourself, and put a date on it that's a few months into the future. Six months is a pretty good stretch. That's the day you're going to open and read the letter.

Chapter 7: Chase the Jeep

- Have you given Jesus the whole room, or are you trying to cram Him in a corner? What do you need to get rid of in your life to make space for Jesus? How would your faith transform if you gave Him the space He wants to be the center of your life?
- Imagine taking everything you pursue—good grades, a better job, a house in a different neighborhood, a boyfriend, whatever—and laying them out on the table. How are these things flowing into your life of faith? Now imagine taking those things one by one and deciding whether you should add them back to your faith and your life. Should you move something from the table to the garbage bin? What would you add back?

Chapter 8: Getting to the "New" Part

- One of the hardest things to believe about God is that He loves you completely and unconditionally. Do you have trouble with this? Is there anything lurking in your heart that says you have to change, be better, or do something different to earn God's love? How would a complete and enduring belief in God's love change your life and fuel your dream?

- What we do with our days will eventually become how we're known and remembered. If you looked at everything on an average Tuesday, what would it say about your faith?
- Fear is a part of all our lives. Even the most fearless among us have to stare it down and decide to act anyway. On a scale of one to ten—with one being "very little" and ten being "all the time"—how much does fear have a hold of your life?
- Knowing your talents is a great starting point for thinking about your dream. Write down ten things about yourself that feel like your innate talents. Maybe you're naturally friendly or optimistic. Maybe you are great at geometry or have a heart for homeless people. Things like this may not seem like "talents" as our culture defines them. They're so innate to who you are that they just feel like second nature. But they *are* your talents. Make a list and give yourself a high five. Oh, and if you're having trouble coming up with ten things, just ask a few people in your life what they think your talents are to give you some hints. My bet is that you'll have a list a lot longer than ten things.
- Some people think their talents are the only thing making up their identity. They lean heavily on them for success or approval. Do you think you've given your talents and gifts too much weight in your sense of self-worth? How could overreliance on your talents give you a "false positive" that you're moving in the direction of your dream?

Chapter 9: Sleepwalking

- Do you live life half awake? Maybe you like routine so much that somewhere along the way you forgot the power of shaking things up a bit. Do you need to become more fully alive?
- If you're a Bible reader, what stands out to you when you think about the miracles in the Bible? What if you believed that God

had a miracle waiting for you too? What would life look like if we peered around every corner, dug in every couch cushion, and looked under the bed to see how God has already been doing miracles for us? Write down a few things that have happened in your life that feel like God's miracles for you.

- Anyone can fall into the trap of thinking that work equals progress. In some sense, I guess that's true if you're doing the right things. Maybe you're so laser-focused on what you want to accomplish that you're grinding yourself into a fine powder with all your hustle. Do you have rhythms in your life that allow you to get adequate rest? Do you sleep enough? Do you work compulsively and realize too late that you're burned out? How can you pursue rest today and this week? How can you build rest into the rhythms of your life?

Chapter 10: One Hundred Calls a Day

- People are essential on the journey to our ambitions. Without others to help, encourage, and support you, it'll be difficult (and probably impossible) to achieve your dream. This can be hard for some people to accept. Are you the kind of person who thinks they need to go it alone? Does help from someone else feel uncomfortable to accept? If so, why?

- List three people in your life to whom you could become more available. What will you do today and this week to make yourself more available in their lives?

- A lot of people are constantly looking at others silently asking the question *What can this person do for me?* It happens in business all the time, and I guess that's okay in some respects. But what about you and your daily life? Are you scanning the room to size up what you can get from the people around you? How would your life change if you flipped the script and instead asked, *What can I give to everyone here?*

Chapter 11: Sea Otters, and
Chapter 12: Finale, and
Chapter 13: Comparison Is a Punk

- Take a moment and list five people in your life who are your friends. Now, as you look at each name, can you remember the last time you asked them a probing question that got past the surface? Now, think about yourself with each of these people. Can you remember the last time you shared something that felt vulnerable and real? In general, would you say you're a person who is willing to go deep with others?

- Does it seem strange or possibly even counterproductive to your dream to think how you can find opportunities for others? Are you afraid that if you give too much there won't be anything left over for yourself?

- Have you ever been in a position to open a path of possibility for someone else? How did it feel to play the role of giver instead of receiver?

- In chapter 13, we talked about the sinister power of comparison. What role does it play in your life? Are you the kind of person who thinks everyone else has it better than you or has it more together than you? List some ways that you struggle to "keep your eyes on your own paper" in your own life.

Part 2: Set Absurd Expectations

Chapter 14: Gather Your Leaves, and
Chapter 15: Sizing Up, and
Chapter 16: Get the Sticks Before the Drums

- Look back to the list of ambitions you started in the last part of this framework. Does your list feel like you, or are there some impostors hanging out in there? Before you move forward in the Dream Big framework, make sure your list is honest and genuine. Your list should feel like an autobiography of who you are and what you *really* want. Revisit your list and revise as needed. Is there anything you need to add or take off? Remember, there are not right or wrong moves here. The only thing that matters is that your list is honest and truly reflects *you*.

- Are there some items on your list that are too vague? If they're not specific enough, you'll never know if you actually achieved them. Go through your list and drill down to get really concrete and specific about your ambitions.

- I'm the kind of guy who has an idea every five seconds. My trouble is not having dreams, but having too many. You might be the same, or you might be the exact opposite. It's all good. If you're going to get some movement on your dreams, you'll have to create some priorities. You can't chase them all at the same time—nor should you. Take the list you have and create three different categories: small, medium, and large. Or if you like coffee, go with Tall, Grande, and Venti. Place everything on your list in one of these categories. Don't worry about doing this exactly right. The exercise is more about clarifying what you can pursue quickly or what might take some time.

- For each of your Venti dreams, answer these three questions:
  - Is it meaningful? (Does this dream reflect my most beautiful values and hopes?)
  - Will it last? (Will this dream stand the test of time? Will it last my lifetime or even past my lifetime?)
  - Will it help others? (Is this dream just another feather in my cap, or will it impact the people around me? Remember, scale doesn't matter—there just needs to be a blast radius of goodness to your dream.)

- Take your list, divided into three categories, and put each item on a single line so they create rows across each category. Now, looking at the "small" dreams, draw a line if one of those dreams seems connected or could lead to a "medium" or "large" dream.
- This is a hard question, but I have to ask. Are you looking to get a pat on your back for some items on your list? Do you want your teacher or pastor to see it so you can feel affirmed? Do you want your spouse or best friend to think you've made the right choices? Be honest. If something on your list feels like someone else's fulfilled expectation of you—but not necessarily a genuine dream of your own—take some time to think about why you added it, then consider if you should take it off your list. The last thing we want is you chasing a dream you think you're supposed to have but don't *actually* have.

Part 3: Explore Opportunities

Chapter 17: Keep the Moon in the Window, and
Chapter 18: The Number for the White House Is (202) 456-1414

- The dreams you wrote down and vetted in the last chapter made it on your list because you haven't accomplished them yet. Why? Are you the kind of person who needs a fully reliable master plan before you take the first step? Are you stopped before you begin because of fear or what others might think? Maybe you have a family or a full-time job and can't carve out the time to make some moves toward your dreams. Take a moment and ask yourself, "What's kept me from pursuing my dreams?" We're not creating solutions for these obstacles just yet. Identifying them, though, is an important step. (We'll get to the solution part later.)

- Think about the body of knowledge you might need to accomplish your dream. Chances are you don't know all that stuff yet. What steps can you take to start learning what you'll need to know when your dream is fully realized?
- Name three people you know right now who could help you make some progress on your dream. Are you willing to approach them and ask for help? If so, how and when will you do that?
- Name three people you *want* to know who can help you toward your dream. Is there a way you can get to them? Can you find their phone number and give them a call? What about their email address? How far are you willing to go to get an audience with someone who could be key for you to accomplish your dream?
- When you look at your list of dreams, take the ones that light you up the most and write down the next action you need to take to get some forward movement. Write only one! It's tempting to write down a sequence of events like lining up dominoes. But I find that it's really empowering to have *one thing* that you can do to move your dream forward. (Of course, once that's done you can write down the next thing. Eventually you'll have a daisy chain of completed steps!)
- Working toward your dreams comes with some opportunity costs. Choosing one dream to chase means you might have to wait on another. So remember to be incredibly picky about how you spend your time, energy, and resources. When you look at your list, is anything sticking out that may not be worth it? Are there one or two large dreams that lead the pack and get you most excited? That's a good sign. Follow the breadcrumb trails to the one or two dreams that get you most excited.

Part 4: Clear the Path

Chapter 19: Hostage Negotiation, and
Chapter 20: Give It a Quarter Twist, and
Chapter 21: Be a Quitter

- This section started with a story about a bank robbery that lead to something we now call Stockholm syndrome. Why do you think we cling to our captors, the things holding us hostage in our lives? As you scan the current dynamics in your life—both internal and external—do you have anything you would say is holding you hostage? If so, how strong is its hold in your life? Take a few minutes to write down some thoughts if you feel you need to name your captors and call them out for the role they play in keeping you hostage.

- Were you raised with any limiting beliefs from your parents? Were you continuously told year after year by a teacher, pastor, coach, or friend what it takes to be accepted? Have you come to believe certain narratives in your life as "universal truths" about who you are? If so, what are those, and where did they come from?

- Now, having identified any limiting beliefs, how might they be standing in the way of some audacious dreams you have or want to have but are too hesitant to chase?

- Have you ever heard the phrase "do it scared"? I heard once that courage isn't the absence of fear but the willingness to act in the face of fear. When you think about the role of fear in your life, what are you willing to do to overcome this emotion when it comes to your big dreams?

- Are there any launching beliefs (the opposite of limiting beliefs) that you can be grateful for and focus on as you make moves toward your dreams? Think of three positive things people have consistently said about you during your life. Maybe you're a natural optimist or selfless or a hard worker. Maybe you have some natural skills and abilities that have consistently caught other people's attention. Create some reminders on sticky notes (or your phone lock screen or written on your bathroom mirror, or wherever you look often) to help you remember what is inherently good and true about you.

• When I've spoken to people about their dreams, one of the most common reasons people tell me their dreams can't happen is all the commitments they currently have and can't let go of. I get it. I've made commitments that seemed good at the time but ended up shackling me to a particular spot. What commitments have you made that take up time, space, and energy on a daily or weekly basis? What would happen if you picked one thing—really, just one—and decided to stop doing it? Maybe it's something as big as a letter of resignation or something as simple as paying for school lunch one day a week instead of packing it. My hunch is you can let go of more than you believe you can. Pick one thing and just see what happens.

• Imagine how much extra time, space, and energy you would have for your dreams if you decided you were in charge of your commitments. I'm not suggesting you ditch everyone and become unreliable. It's important to keep your word. But you also have permission to change and shift, to adapt and be nimble. Describe a day in the near future when you've dropped some of the burdens you're currently carrying and replaced them with activities that move you closer to a fulfilled dream.

• Thursday is coming. It happens every week, so you know you can rely on it. Name one thing you're going to quit this Thursday. It could be a chore or a job or a daily routine. It could be a volunteer position or a habit or negative attitude. It could be anything, really, just something you decide isn't helping you anymore. Go ahead—write down your own thing, then mark your calendar for this Thursday. It's quitting time!

- Saying no is not a pleasant experience for most people. But it's a critical skill if you're going to save space for your dreams. Often, we just need a little practice saying no. Go practice saying no one hundred times in the bathroom mirror. Get a few close friends together and have a "no" party where you practice with each other. Step out on your front porch and yell it at the top of your lungs. Think of a few common occurrences in your life where you just can't seem to say no. Now, make a plan to decline the next time. The truth is, people respect it when you tell them no in the right way, like we discussed in the chapter. It really is a liberating and powerful tool on your journey toward your dream.

Part 5: Take Action

Chapter 22: Living on the Edge of Yikes, and
Chapter 23: 10:34–10:35, and
Chapter 24: One Thousand Words a Day

- It's natural to seek comfort and familiarity in life. A life filled with uncertainty can feel too chaotic and stressful. Just the right amount of stress, however, can awaken our senses and bring out some of our best traits. This tension is almost always part of chasing a dream. How about you? Are you afraid of living on the edge of yikes? Does it get you completely amped and ready to take on the world? How would you describe your default reaction as you start to take some steps toward your dreams?

- You might be able to divide the world between people who procrastinate and those who don't. It's the late-night crammers before the big test versus the people who studied for weeks. Be honest with yourself—are you a procrastinator? Do you think of a dozen reasons why not to get started? Decide now how you're going to respond as you take your first steps toward a dream.

- Sometimes the resistance we feel toward action comes from inside us. Other times it comes from the people around us. Can you name one or two people who you think will try to tamp down your dream? How will you respond when they start to douse your attempts?

- I shared a few ideas to help you get some concrete plans to move toward your dream: make a date with yourself, make one phone call a day, set incremental milestones, and so on. Go back through the list and focus on a few that resonate with you. (Or, if you have a few tricks and tactics you already use, think about those.) Make a list of some things you want to do and decide in advance when and how you're going to do them. Put them on your calendar. Have a friend call you to check that you actually did it. Whatever it takes, decide now that you're going to act.

- Perfectionism can be a major roadblock to our dreams. We think, *If I can't do it exactly how I want, I won't do it at all.* Don't fall prey to this. Are you a perfectionist who does less because it won't be exactly right the first time?

- Fear of failure is another big reason I hear from people struggling to realize their dreams. What if you failed on purpose just to get it out of your system? The truth is, failure is a reality for all of us. You might as well join the club and realize that not every attempt toward your dream will be successful. The real challenge is this: how will you respond to failure? Take a few minutes and write a paragraph or two about how you'll respond when things don't go as planned.

Part 6: Expect Setbacks

Chapter 25: Pick the Vespa over the Harley, and
Chapter 26: Three Epic Fails

- The place where faith and failure meet can be tricky. You've probably heard people say "God opened the door" or "God closed the door." Maybe you're one of them. It's tempting to interpret our setbacks as heavenly signals we're headed in the wrong direction. I don't think this is true, because the dreams we have, I believe, are God-given gifts. How about you? Do you tend to think any blip along the way is God speaking to you in code? If so, why?

- I told a story about Sweet Maria after our Lodge burned down. I learned something powerful and precious about her in the wake of that loss. It made the catastrophe worth every singed beam and piece of timber. Have you experienced some setbacks and simply tried to power through or get past the pain as quickly as possible? Take a moment and sit in the heap. What can you learn about yourself that only setbacks can help reveal?

- Sometimes our setbacks make us more qualified, not less. Think about your life and some attempts that didn't go as planned. Maybe you faceplanted or lost some money or hurt someone you cared about. But with a little distance from the setback, you also gained some authority to help others avoid the same. Can you recall a time in your life when a difficult experience equipped you to help someone else avoid the same mistake? Can you recall a time when a past setback helped *you* avoid the same mistake?

- How would you describe your relationship with failure? Do you avoid it at all costs? If so, why? What do you fear about failing?

- Faith and friendship are essential tools to keep us motivated when we face a major setback toward our dreams. Have an emergency kit of these ready when it happens to you. Do you have some favorite Bible verses God has used in your life to keep your head up? Is there a close friend or two who has a knack for encouraging you when times get tough? Put those verses and those names in a special place. When you've hit a roadblock on your Dream Big journey, get those out. Read. Make the call. Don't be afraid to reach for some encouragement and truth exactly when you need it.

Part 7: Sustain Belief and Land the Plane

Chapter 27: Check Your Ropes, and
Chapter 28: Ground Effect, and
Chapter 29: Matters of the Heart

- Are you securely tied into your faith and relationships? Think hard about this. Can you really rely on them when you're dangling from a cliff face? If you need to tighten some knots or click into some carabiners in your relationship with God, do it. If you need to reconnect more firmly with the people you depend on most, don't wait another second. List three ways you can get more secure and do these things.

- When you are chasing an ambition, it can take you into uncharted territory. You might not know anyone who's attempted the thing you're trying to accomplish. If that's the case, you should take it as a signal that you're on the right track. Take a few minutes and reconnect with your vision. Write down in exquisite detail what will happen when you've made it a reality. Who will it help? What would an average Tuesday look and feel like when you're living out your dream?

- When you face a setback, it's normal and natural to get into a funk. The problem comes when we stay there too long. What's your tendency? Are you able to acknowledge a difficult spot you're in and find a way forward? Or does it become your new return address? One of my favorite ways to overcome a setback is to preplan what I'll do when it happens. Do the same. Think of three things you'll do when you face a setback. It may not completely change your situation, but it will change you. And that's the starting point for moving forward.

- I'm an impatient guy. All my friends and family know this. As I've chased some of my dreams, though, I've experienced how patience is a powerful tool for the journey. What about you? Do you know your sweet spot between abdication and expectant waiting? Sometimes it's hard to recognize, but think about it. What does purposeful waiting look like in your own life?

- If you've been fully engaged in this process of discovery and self-reflection, my hunch is that you've covered quite a bit of distance so far. Take a moment to reflect on where you started and where you are now. Do you have more clarity? More energy? I know it's hard work sometimes, which is why you should stop right now and congratulate yourself for everything you've poured into this. Remember, you're worth it. Take five minutes and write down what you're proud of in this process.

- One of the head-fakes we get as we pursue our most beautiful ambitions is thinking we have to go from step one to step twenty-three in one major leap. Don't fall for it. Revisit your lists from earlier in the book—your list of dreams and the opportunities you're going to explore—and star the ones that feel like small things that can lead to big things.

- As you've gone through this book and the prompts in this section, maybe you've tried a few new things along the way. How has it gone? Have you gotten a bit of lift-off, or are you still on the cusp of making some moves? This is a critical moment. Go back and reread the "Pitch, pick, and point" section of chapter 28. How can you do the same in your journey?

- Something is better than nothing, right? I think this is almost always true. When it comes to your dreams, I *know* it's always true. As you move toward your dream, remember to celebrate even the small wins and half-steps forward. What are some midway points you can celebrate? Go buy yourself a few medals or write yourself some notes of congratulations to open when you've made some progress.
- Remember learning that thing in school where an object in motion tends to stay in motion and an object at rest tends to stay at rest? Much of the Dream Big framework is to help you move from rest to motion. As you land the plane on this process, don't overlook the feeling of excitement and momentum you get from making some moves forward. As you end this book and look out to the life in front of you, stop and take a deep breath. Tell yourself, "I am going to do this." Hopefully you've identified a few dreams you're going to take some action on. Write down this phrase for each one of them "I will [fill in the blank with your dream(s)]."

ACKNOWLEDGMENTS

A special thanks to the Love Does and Bob teams: Dae, Jody, Becky, Haley, Tatave, Jennifer, Ashton, Catherine, Grace, Scott, and our amazing interns. Thank you for being so busy doing impossible things in war-torn countries around the world. You haven't stopped to figure out what you are doing should not have been possible. Your dreams, ambitions, and capabilities have both dwarfed and shaped mine.

Thank you to Sweet Maria, Lindsey, Jon, Richard, Ashley, Adam, Kaitlyn, and all of the people they love most. Their constant support and wisdom are the main reasons this book actually got finished.

You also heard about Bryan Norman in these pages. He has been the guy behind the curtain making all of the words happen in every one of my books and is the reason most of them are spelled correctly and make sense. He's a bright light who shies away from all the spotlights, but you need to know some of my best ideas are really his.

To Thomas Nelson and the Nelson Books team, thank you for giving me the chance to be an author and for making me look way better than I deserve. A special thanks to Timothy Paulson, Webb

Younce, Jamie Lockard, Janene MacIvor, Rachel Tockstein, Karen Jackson, Belinda Bass, and Kristen Golden.

To the team at The Oaks—Jamie, Paulo, Stefanie, Justin, Heidi, Darrell, Mago, and my buddy Miles Adcox—and to the teams at OnSite, Pepperdine, and Young Life's Malibu, your commitment to others and how your dreams inform your excellence inspire me every day.

Finally, to the students in our Love Does schools around the world in Uganda, Somalia, India, Nepal, Afghanistan, and a few countries we can't mention yet, thank you for courageously leading us with love. Your ambitions for your lives have become ours.

ABOUT THE AUTHOR

Bob is the longest-serving volunteer at Love Does and is its chief balloon inflator. He calls himself a "recovering lawyer" because after practicing law for almost thirty years, he walked into his own law firm and quit in order to pursue encouraging people full time. Bob is driven by a desire to love people and to motivate others to do the same. These days, you'll find Bob in an airport on his way to connect with and encourage people or, more likely, on his way home for supper with Sweet Maria.

A few years ago, Bob wrote a book called *Everybody, Always*. Before that, he wrote one called *Love Does*. He gave away all the proceeds from that book to help change the lives of children in countries where armed conflicts had left them vulnerable. Today, Love Does is an organization dedicated to helping kids in these areas, including Uganda, Somalia, Afghanistan, Nepal, and India. You can find out more about Love Does at www.LoveDoes.org.

CONNECT WITH BOB

Bob's passion is people. He'd love to hear from you if you want to email him at info@bobgoff.com. You can also follow him on Instagram and Twitter, @bobgoff.

Here's his cell phone number if you want to give him a call: (619) 985-4747.

Bob is a personal coach. You can find out more at coachingwithbobgoff.com. He is also available to inspire and engage your team, organization, or audience. To date, he's spoken to more than two million people, bringing his unique perspective and exciting storytelling with him. If you're interested in having Bob come to your event, check out bobgoff.com/speaking.

New Video Study for Your Church or Small Group

If you've enjoyed this book, now you can go deeper with the companion video Bible study!

In this five-session study, Bob Goff helps you apply the principles in *Dream Big* to your life. The study guide includes video notes, group discussion questions, and personal study and reflection materials for in-between sessions.

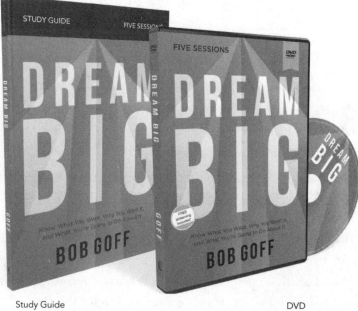

Study Guide
9780310121329

DVD
9780310121343

Available now at your favorite bookstore,
or streaming video on StudyGateway.com.

THOMAS NELSON
Since 1798

ALSO AVAILABLE FROM BOB GOFF

Just imagine what God could do with a group of people who were passionate about Jesus' love and eager to put it into practice. Just think how this could impact the world! In *Love Does*, we'll explore how God's love is active, takes risks, and changes things. In a word, how God's love...does.

Video Bible Study Also Available

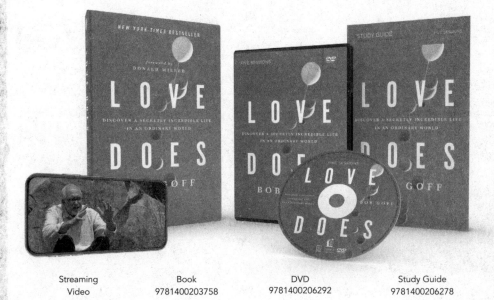

| Streaming Video | Book 9781400203758 | DVD 9781400206292 | Study Guide 9781400206278 |

ALSO AVAILABLE FROM BOB GOFF

Driven by Bob's trademark storytelling, *Everybody, Always* reveals the lessons Bob learned–often the hard way–about what it means to love without inhibition, insecurity, or restriction. From finding the right friends to discovering the upside of failure, *Everybody Always* points the way to embodying love by doing the unexpected, the intimidating, the seemingly impossible.

Video Bible Study Also Available

| Streaming Video | Book 9780718078133 | DVD 9780310095361 | Study Guide 9780310095330 |

THOMAS NELSON
Since 1798